New York Bucket List Adventure Guide

Explore 100 Offbeat Destinations You Must Visit!

Casey Wood

Canyon Press
canyon@purplelink.org

Please consider writing a review!
Just visit: purplelink.org/review

ISBN: 978-1-957590-22-6

FREE BONUS

Discover 31 Incredible Places You Can
Visit Next! Just Go To:

purplelink.org/travel

Table of Contents:

How to Use This Book

Welcome to your very own adventure guide to exploring the many wonders of the state of New York. Not only does this book offer the most wonderful places to visit and sights to see in the vast state, but it provides GPS coordinates for Google Maps to make exploring that much easier.

Adventure Guide

Sorted by region, this guide offers over 100 amazing wonders found in New York for you to see and explore. They can be visited in any order and this book will help you keep track of where you've been and where to look forward to going next. Each section describes the area or place, what to look for, Physical Address, and what you may need to bring along.

GPS Coordinates

As you can imagine, not all of the locations in this book have a physical address. Fortunately, some of our listed wonders are either located within a National Park or Reserve, or near a city, town, or place of business. For those that are not associated with a specific location, it is easiest to map it using GPS coordinates.

Luckily, Google has a system of codes that converts the coordinates into pin-drop locations that Google Maps can interpret and navigate.

Each adventure in this guide includes GPS coordinates along with a physical address whenever it is available.

It is important that you are prepared for poor cell signals. It is recommended that you route your location and ensure that the directions are accessible offline. Depending on your device and the distance of some locations, you may need to travel with a backup battery source.

About New York

Located in the northeastern United States, New York is well-known as the home of New York City, Niagara Falls, Adirondack Park, and the Statue of Liberty. This state is also famous for its high cost of living, diverse geography, innovation, and bustling economy. Its nickname is the Empire State.

In 1624, the Dutch first settled the area on the Hudson River. Two years later, they established the colony of New Amsterdam on what is now Manhattan Island. In 1664, the English seized the area, renaming it New York. New York was one of the original 13 colonies to declare independence from Great Britain in 1776.

After the Constitution was ratified in 1788, New York City became the first capital of the United States. George Washington was sworn in as the first president at Federal Hall, located on Wall Street, on April 30, 1789.

Albany was established as the state capital of New York in 1797. Prior to that date, the capital was moved several times between the cities of Poughkeepsie, Albany, Kingston, New York City, and Hurley. Albany is one of the longest-surviving settlements from the original 13 colonies and the oldest continuously chartered city in the United States.

There are 57 counties that comprise the state of New York. With 24 national parks within its borders, the state is a popular resort destination with vast numbers of mountains available for skiing in the winter. Some famous icons who trace their roots to New York include Robert Downey Jr.,

Michael Jordan, Tom Cruise, Jennifer Lopez, Mark Zuckerberg, and Lady Gaga.

New York is also known for being home to the National Baseball Hall of Fame, Times Square, Central Park, the Adirondacks, and the Catskills.

Landscape and Climate

New York is broken up between highlands and lowlands. The highlands include the Adirondacks in the northeast, the Allegheny Plateau and Catskills along the southern border with Pennsylvania, and the Taconic Mountains and Hudson Highlands that border several New England states.

The lowlands include the Hudson and Champlain valleys to the east, the Lake Ontario Lowlands and the Mohawk Valley stretching across the central interior, and other relatively flat regions such as the St. Lawrence Valley, Long Island, the Lake Erie Plain, and the Susquehanna Valley. Most residents of the state live in these low-lying areas.

New York is located in a temperate zone, meaning it experiences all four seasons. Winters can be snowy and cold, while summers can be steamy and hot. Spring can be very unpredictable with snow one day and warm breezes the next.

Brooklyn Botanic Garden

The Brooklyn Botanic Garden offers 52 acres of natural beauty and features over 18,000 types of plants from all around the world. It houses plants from all seasons as well as indoor tropical plants and bonsais. Visitors can expect to spend 2 to 3 hours here.

The garden was founded in 1910, although the area was initially barren. Frederick Jr. and John Charles Olmsted designed the original garden. However, the current version is largely due to Harold Caparn, who took over the project in 1912. Visitors can have their private events hosted and catered at the Palm House and Atrium.

Best Time to Visit: The Brooklyn Botanic Garden is open year round.

Pass/Permit/Fees: Admission is $18 for adults, $12 for seniors over 65, and $12 for students 12 and up. Children under 12, members, and guests with community tickets may enter for free.

Closest City or Town: Brooklyn

Physical Address:
Brooklyn Botanic Garden
990 Washington Avenue
Brooklyn, NY 11225

GPS Coordinates: 40.67033° N, 73.96247° W

Did You Know? It typically takes visitors about 3 to 4 hours to walk through the garden.

Brooklyn Bridge Love Locks

Love locks are padlocks that couples place on something such as the Brooklyn Bridge before throwing away the key as a way of symbolizing their unbreakable bond. In addition to the bridge, people have been known to put their locks on benches and light poles.

New York City officials made a public announcement in 2016 that they would no longer tolerate the addition of locks to the Brooklyn Bridge. All previously added locks were removed. However, couples still go on the bridge and add their locks despite warnings of fines from the authorities.

Best Time to Visit: The Brooklyn Bridge is open year round.

Pass/Permit/Fees: There is no fee to visit the bridge.

Closest City or Town: Brooklyn

Physical Address:
Brooklyn Bridge
New York, NY 10038

GPS Coordinates: 40.70643° N, 73.99683° W

Did You Know? If too many locks are added to a streetlight, the combined weight can collapse the fixture. Because of this, officials remove locks added to streetlights on the Brooklyn Bridge while leaving the ones attached to the physical bridge.

Coney Island History Project

Founded in 2004, the Coney Island History Project is a nonprofit organization intended to create awareness of Coney Island's colorful history and encourage appreciation of its neighborhood today. The project's public programs began in 2005 with the opening of the Coney Island Hall of Fame and Coney Island Voices. In 2011, the project moved to its current home on West 12th Street behind the Wonder Wheel. They collect and archive oral histories through interviews. Visitors can both listen to and record submissions for these archives. Many of the oral histories of departed Coney Island luminaries have been preserved by the project, including those of Jack Rollino, Jimmy McCullough, Jack Ward, Matt Kennedy, and others. They offer unique walking tours year round.

Best Time to Visit: The Coney Island History Project is open year round.

Pass/Permit/Fees: Visiting the Exhibition Center is free; walking tour tickets are $25

Closest City or Town: Brooklyn

Physical Address:
Coney Island History Project
3059 W. 12th Street
Brooklyn, NY 11224

GPS Coordinates: 40.58714° N, 73.97954° W

Did You Know? The Exhibition Center features a toll house sign from 1823.

Deno's Wonder Wheel

Deno's Wonder Wheel is a New York City landmark. It was conceived by Charles Hermann and built in 1920 by the Eccentric Ferris Wheel Company. The ride stands 150 feet tall and weighs 200 tons. It has 24 cars, 8 that are stationary and 16 of which can swing. The swinging cars are on a serpentine track, moving toward the hub of the wheel as it turns. Each car holds up to 6 people for a maximum capacity of 144 riders.

The Wonder Wheel has a perfect safety record. Every year it is overhauled and painted to protect it from the weather as well as wear and tear.

Best Time to Visit: The Wonder Wheel is open from April 10 through October 31.

Pass/Permit/Fees: Admission to the park is free, but you must buy credits to go on rides. It costs $40 for 50 ride credits, $70 for 100 ride credits, or $100 for 150 ride credits.

Closest City or Town: Brooklyn

Physical Address:
Deno's Wonder Wheel Amusement Park
3059 W. 12th Street
Brooklyn, NY 11224

GPS Coordinates: 40.57418° N, 73.97920° W

Did You Know? Deno's Wonder Wheel is constructed from Bethlehem steel that was forged right on Coney Island Beach.

House of Wax

The House of Wax is a museum-bar combination. Most of the objects displayed are remnants of a forgotten exhibition known as *Castan's Panopticum*. *Castan's Panopticum* displayed anatomical and pathological waxworks, death masks of murderers and celebrities, anatomical Venuses, waxes showing the effects of syphilis, and curiosities like mummies, monkey skeletons, and stuffed alligators. Live acts were also presented with dancers, singers, and ventriloquists.

Panoptica exhibits did not survive past the 1930s for various reasons, including their association with lower cultural status. House of Wax is an attempt to evoke and revive the atmosphere of *Castan's Panopticum*. The majority of waxes are drawn from that collection, while additional artifacts come from other private collections.

Best Time to Visit: House of Wax is open year round.

Pass/Permit/Fees: There is no cost for admission, but bring money if you intend to have a drink at the bar.

Closest City or Town: Brooklyn

Physical Address:
House of Wax
445 Albee Square West #4410
Brooklyn, NY 11201

GPS Coordinates: 40.69185° N, 73.98287° W

Did You Know? House of Wax is combined with the Alamo Drafthouse, which is also a movie theater.

House of Yes

House of Yes is a creative collective and nightclub in Brooklyn. It grew out of NYC's Burning Man and Do-It-Yourself scenes. The nightclub is known for burlesque dancers, wild parties with strange themes, and circus performers. House of Yes also hosts immersive cinema and creative experiences that transcend genre and defy categorization.

Internationally, it has received recognition for holding the culture of nightlife to a higher standard with its dedication to consent culture, nurturing emerging performance artists, and fostering self-expression.

Best Time to Visit: House of Yes is open Wednesday through Sunday during the evenings.

Pass/Permit/Fees: Ticket prices vary based on when you purchase them and the event you intend to see. The earlier you purchase a ticket, the cheaper it will be.

Closest City or Town: Brooklyn

Physical Address:
House of Yes
2 Wyckoff Avenue
Brooklyn, NY 11237

GPS Coordinates: 40.70768° N, 73.92373° W

Did You Know? The creators of House of Yes opened a spin-off club called House of X in Manhattan.

New York Transit Museum

The New York Transit Museum in downtown Brooklyn displays historical artifacts of the city bus lines, commuter rail systems, and NYC subway. It is an authentic subway station that was decommissioned in 1936. The museum highlights the public transportation network, including construction equipment, the typography in the stations, and vintage subway cars.

The museum offers a program of films, tours, seminars, and lectures for all ages. In addition, there are off-site programs that consist of guided tours of artwork and architecture, subway stations, MTA facilities, and New York neighborhoods.

Best Time to Visit: The New York Transit Museum is open year round.

Pass/Permit/Fees: Admission is $10 for adults, $5 for seniors ages 62 and up, and $5 for children ages 2–12.

Closest City or Town: Brooklyn

Physical Address:
New York Transit Museum
99 Schermerhorn Street
Brooklyn, NY 11201

GPS Coordinates: 40.69625° N, 73.99053° W

Did You Know? The New York Transit Museum has a gift shop and gallery annex at the Grand Central Terminal. It also has a gift shop in Lower Manhattan at 2 Broadway that features MTA-themed iconic gifts.

Eternal Flame Falls

Eternal Flame Falls is located within Chestnut Ridge Park in a secluded area away from the crowds. Visitors should be wary of the path to the falls as it can get quite muddy and is filled with obstacles. Additionally, when walking upstream at Shale Creek, if the falls are overflowing, visitors' feet will get wet.

The smell of rotten eggs is noticeable near the ravine where the falls are located. This is the result of natural gas seeping through rock fissures from layers of Hanover shale. One such fissure is located behind the falls in a grotto. Because of its location, it can sustain being lit, hence the name Eternal Flame Falls. The 30-foot waterfall is dependent on rain and snow melt to maintain the water flow.

Best Time to Visit: The best time to visit Eternal Flame Falls is in early spring, especially right after a bout of heavy rain.

Pass/Permit/Fees: There is no fee associated with this location.

Closest City or Town: Buffalo

Physical Address:
Eternal Flame Hiking Trailhead Parking
Chestnut Ridge Road
Orchard Park, NY 14127

GPS Coordinates: 42.70267° N, 78.74766° W

Did You Know? It is theorized that the natural gas is coming from 1,300 feet below the surface.

Historic Colored Musicians Club

The only remaining club of its kind, the Historic Colored Musicians Club was designated a historical preservation site in 1999. In 2018, it was designated as a National Historic Site.

Currently, the club promotes the preservation and historical research of jazz in Buffalo. The youth of the community can receive free jazz lessons from the club members. On Sunday evenings, the members hold a jam session.

Several jazz giants were known to have played at the Historic Colored Musicians Club, including Duke Ellington, Dizzy Gillespie, and Miles Davis.

Best Time to Visit: The Historic Colored Musicians Club is open year-round.

Pass/Permit/Fees: Fees vary based on performance. Some are free while others have rates based on age or membership.

Closest City or Town: Buffalo

Physical Address:
Colored Musicians Club
145 Broadway
Buffalo, NY 14203

GPS Coordinates: 42.88736° N, 78.86785° W

Did You Know? The Historic Colored Musicians Club is the longest continuously running Black-owned club in the U.S.

Michigan Street African American Heritage

The Michigan Street African American Heritage Corridor is recognized nationally and internationally as a central point for learning about Black history in Buffalo. In the corridor, people can visit stops on the Underground Railroad, learn about those who shaped the abolitionist and civil rights movements, and enjoy some jazz history. It includes such popular locations as the Colored Musicians Club, the Nash House Museum, the Michigan Street Baptist Church, and the WUFO Black Radio History Collective. Tours can be taken by reaching out to one of the anchor properties such as the Colored Musicians Club.

Best Time to Visit: The corridor is open Saturdays from 10 a.m. to 2 p.m. by appointment.

Pass/Permit/Fees: Adult admission is $15 for an in-person or guided virtual tour and $5 for a self-guided virtual tour. Children may visit for free.

Closest City or Town: Buffalo

Physical Address:
Michigan Street African American Heritage Corridor
Michigan Avenue
Buffalo, NY 14203

GPS Coordinates: 42.88707° N, 78.86749° W

Did You Know? The city of Buffalo is making major investments in the corridor to promote it as a tourist destination.

Bronck Family and Farmstead

The Bronck Museum features perhaps the longest-surviving home in upstate New York. Pieter Bronck constructed a one-room house in 1663, and his grandson enlarged it in 1738. The enlargement featured typical Dutch architecture characteristics like parapet gables and sloping dormers.

The home and surrounding farmstead belonged to the Bronck family for eight generations. It was donated in 1938 to the Historical Society of Greene County.

Today, the rooms have 18th-century woodwork and feature many items from the Bronck family. Outbuildings include three barns (one of which was the state's first 13-sided barn) and a 19th-century kitchen dependency. There are also displays of wheeled vehicles, sleighs, and agricultural tools.

Best Time to Visit: The Bronck Museum is open Thursdays and Fridays from 11 a.m. to 2 p.m.

Pass/Permit/Fees: Admission is $8 per person.

Closest City or Town: Catskill

Physical Address:
Bronck Family Farmstead
90 County Route 42
Coxsackie, NY 12051

GPS Coordinates: 42.34700° N, 73.84467° W

Did You Know? Pieter and his wife Hilletje were failed owners of a tavern and brewery before they founded their homestead.

Kaaterskill Falls

Kaaterskill Falls, the tallest cascading waterfall in the state, drops 260 feet in two tiers. The location was considered sacred by the Mohican people as the resting place of the creator. Kaaterskill Falls has been featured in poetry, paintings, films, and photography. One of the most notable stories that takes place at this location is Washington Irving's *Rip Van Winkle*.

The falls are in the Catskill Mountains between the hamlets of Palenville and Haines Falls in Green County. The COVID-19 pandemic drove up the number of visitors as people sought an outdoor escape. The state has invested over $750,000 in safety improvements in the area following several accidental deaths.

Best Time to Visit: Kaaterskill Falls is open year round.

Pass/Permit/Fees: There is no fee to visit this location.

Closest City or Town: Catskill

Physical Address:
Laurel House Trail, Kaaterskill Falls Viewing Platform
103 Laurel House Road
Palenville, NY 12463

GPS Coordinates: 42.22159° N, 74.06579° W

Did You Know? In one of his most famous paintings, Thomas Cole placed a lone warrior watching over Kaaterskill Falls as a testament to the area's wild beauty.

Cherry Plain State Park

Cherry Plain State Park is located 19 miles southeast of Grafton in the woods of the Taconic Valley. The park features 175 acres set on Black River Pond, which has a sandy beach, adjacent picnic grounds, and a boat launch. There are also bridle paths, biking and hiking routes, and nature trails that serve as cross-country ski trails in the winter.

Anglers can fish for pickerel, bass, and bullheads. Another special feature of the park is the trail that leads to the Charcoal Kiln Site. It begins at the southern corner of the main parking lot. Nearby attractions include Schodack Island State Park, Bennington Battlefield State Historic Site, and Peebles Island State Park.

Best Time to Visit: Cherry Plain State Park is open year round.

Pass/Permit/Fees: Admission is $7 per person. For overnight camping, fees are $12–$19 for residents or $17–$24 for nonresidents.

Closest City or Town: Cherry Plain

Physical Address:
Cherry Plain State Park
10 State Park Road
Petersburg, NY 12138

GPS Coordinates: 42.63323° N, 73.40424° W

Did You Know? The Capital District Wildlife Management Area surrounds the park.

Brace Mountain

Brace Mountain is located at the southeastern border of New York where Connecticut and Massachusetts meet. It sits within Taconic State Park. The high point on Brace is 2,311 feet, the highest point in Duchess County. This mountain marks the watershed divide of the Housatonic and Hudson rivers. On clear days, hikers will be rewarded with exceptional views of Mount Greylock to the northeast, the Catskill Mountains to the west, Bear Mountain to the west, the Helderberg Escarpment near Albany to the northwest, the Hudson Highlands to the south, and the Housatonic State Forest to the southeast. In the Taconic State Park, visitors can camp, bike, swim, seasonally hunt, hike, snowshoe, and cross-country ski.

Best Time to Visit: The best time to visit is in spring, summer, or fall.

Pass/Permit/Fees: There is no fee to visit this location.

Closest City or Town: Copake

Physical Address:
Brace Mountain
12-2 Altenburg Road
Millerton, NY 12546

GPS Coordinates: 42.04539° N, 73.49253° W

Did You Know? The tripoint of Connecticut, Massachusetts, and New York lies on an unmarked path approximately 0.3 miles to the northeast of Brace's summit. A large stone marker identifies the exact point.

Taconic State Park

Taconic State Park is on the borders between New York, Connecticut, and Massachusetts. It even features a trail, known as the Bash Bish Trail, that takes hikers across. This part runs along 16 miles of the Taconic Mountains and features two developed areas: Rudd Pond and Copake Falls. These both offer extensive trail systems with something for every level of hiker.

Year-round activities are available, including cross-country skiing, snowshoeing, and snowmobiling in the winter. During the spring and summer, visitors can fish, swim, hike, and bike. Hunting is also allowed according to state hunting regulations.

Best Time to Visit: Taconic State Park is open year round.

Pass/Permit/Fees: Admission is $8 for cars, $35 for nonprofit buses, and $75 for commercial buses.

Closest City or Town: Copake

Physical Address:
Taconic State Park
253 NY-344
Copake Falls, NY 12517

GPS Coordinates: 42.12201° N, 73.51981° W

Did You Know? The park features the Copake Iron Works Museum, one of the most complete iron works in the four-state Litchfield Iron District.

Cooperstown

Settled in the late 18th century, Cooperstown is a small rural town that's full of restored buildings and cultural attractions that visitors will remember for a long time. It's home to the National Baseball Hall of Fame, established in 1939 in an effort to drive tourist traffic back to Cooperstown after it was hit hard by the Great Depression.

An expanded library and research facility was opened in addition to the Hall of Fame in 1994. Cooperstown also features the Farmer's Museum, which is one of the oldest rural-life museums in the country. Visitors can experience 19th-century rural life through demonstrations and interactive exhibits. The Glimmerglass Festival is a summer opera festival performed overlooking Otsego Lake.

Best Time to Visit: The best time to visit Cooperstown is in the spring and summer.

Pass/Permit/Fees: There is no fee associated with just visiting the town; however, different activities will have varying fees.

Closest City or Town: Fly Creek

Physical Address:
Cooperstown, NY 13326

GPS Coordinates: 42.69909° N, 74.928687° W

Did You Know? Cooperstown is home to the world's only baseball wax museum.

Balsam Mountain

Balsam Mountain features a loop hike that can be done in either a clockwise or counterclockwise direction. Moderate in ability, it offers a long summit walk with a great viewpoint. Numerous stream crossings throughout the hike are fun in the summer but can be a concern for hikers in the winter months.

This mountain is one of 35 peaks in the Catskill Mountains that exceeds 3,500 feet in elevation. Under appropriate conditions during the winter, it can be an ideal spot for a snowshoe hike.

Most of the upper forest of Balsam Mountain remains in first growth, meaning that it has never been logged or otherwise exploited.

Best Time to Visit: The best time to visit Balsam Mountain is March through October.

Pass/Permit/Fees: There is no fee to visit this location.

Closest City or Town: Fleischmanns

Physical Address:
Balsam, Rider Hollow Trailhead Parking
Unnamed Road (off Todd Mountain Road)
Arkville, NY 12406

GPS Coordinates: 42.10499° N, 74.51739° W

Did You Know? While most of the mountain is publicly owned and managed, the summit is on a small section of private land.

Letchworth State Park

The Genesee River travels through the gorge of Letchworth State Park and over three large waterfalls between cliffs that are as high as 550 feet in some places. There are 66 miles of hiking trails to choose from. Additionally, there are trails available for biking, cross-country skiing, horseback riding, and snowmobiling.

Letchworth offers history, performing arts, and nature programs in addition to a summer lecture series, kayaking, whitewater rafting, a pool for swimming, guided walks, and hot-air ballooning. In the winter, visitors can go snow tubing, snowmobiling, and cross-country skiing. The park includes roughly 17 miles of wilderness that encompass 14,350 acres.

Best Time to Visit: The best time to visit Letchworth State Park is October.

Pass/Permit/Fees: Admission is $8 per vehicle, or you can purchase an annual state park pass for $65. Entry fees for buses range from $35 to $75.

Closest City or Town: Geneseo

Physical Address:
Letchworth State Park
1 Letchworth State Park
Castile, NY 14427

GPS Coordinates: 42.67382° N, 77.97041° W

Did You Know? Letchworth State Park is known as the Grand Canyon of the East.

Stony Brook State Park

Stony Brook State Park features three large waterfalls and at least six smaller ones. During the summer months, the creek is dammed in two places to create a natural swimming area. After the Civil War, the park was opened to the public for only a small admission fee. In 1883, a railroad bridge was constructed over the gorge, and a station was built in Dansville. This brought tourists by the thousands, with the 1920s seeing the largest crowds.

When the Great Depression hit, the private park began to struggle, so in 1928, the state took over. The Civilian Conservation Corps made a major effort in the 1930s to rebuild the park infrastructure and expand it to almost 600 acres.

Best Time to Visit: The best time to visit Stony Brook State Park is in the spring, summer, or fall.

Pass/Permit/Fees: Admission is $9 for cars, $35 for nonprofit buses, $75 for commercial buses, or $75 for a seasonal bus pass.

Closest City or Town: Geneseo

Physical Address:
Stony Brook State Park
10820 NY-36
Dansville, NY 14437

GPS Coordinates: 42.52586° N, 77.69600° W

Did You Know? The campground office is located where the railroad station used to be.

Herkimer Diamond Mines

There are three diamond mines at the Herkimer Diamond Mines. The diamonds found here are short and stubby with a hardiness of 7.5. Visitors will need to dress according to the forecast since the weather is highly unpredictable. For those planning on mining, it is recommended that they wear safety goggles, jeans, a long-sleeve shirt, and close-toed shoes. The three mines are all surface mines and completely open, so visitors will not have to worry about navigating any underground tunnels. In addition to hammering rocks, many people will successfully find diamonds by scavenging. The Minor's Village is comprised of a Town Hall, Canteen Café, Prospector Pete's Panning Place, Trading Post, Build and Share Activity Center, and Rock Hound Academy Learning Center.

Best Time to Visit: Most areas of Herkimer Diamond Mines are open from 9 a.m. to 5 p.m. daily.

Pass/Permit/Fees: Admission is $14 for guests ages 13 and up, $12 for children ages 5–12, and free for children under 5.

Closest City or Town: Herkimer

Physical Address:
Herkimer Diamond Mines
4601 NY-28
Herkimer, NY 13350

GPS Coordinates: 42.12397° N, 74.97953° W

Did You Know? Herkimer diamonds are double-terminated quartz crystals.

Point Au Roche State Park

Located on the northwestern shore of Lake Champlain, Point Au Roche State Park is a combination of cleared and undeveloped areas that features a beach and picnic facilities. Boating, fishing, volleyball, and softball are among the most popular activities with visitors. The Nature Center, which is available to the public all year, offers many programs as well. The park also features multiple trails for visitors to hike and bike on. They are used all year long for school programs, cross-country skiing, and nature hikes. Boaters are asked to hook to available mooring lines. A staff member will approach in a boat for registration and to collect mooring fees.

Best Time to Visit: The best time to visit Point Au Roche State Park is from May to November.

Pass/Permit/Fees: Admission is $7 for the beach or $6 for non-beach areas, $35 for nonprofit buses, and $75 for commercial buses. Mooring fees are $17 with a weekend or holiday surcharge of $4. Out-of-state boaters must pay an additional $5.

Closest City or Town: Ingraham

Physical Address:
Point Au Roche State Park
19 Camp Red Cloud Road
Plattsburgh, NY 12901

GPS Coordinates: 44.78616° N, 73.38189° W

Did You Know? Anglers can fish for tiger muskellunge, muskellunge, kokanee salmon, and splake at the park.

Taughannock Falls State Park

Taughannock Falls State Park is named for the waterfall that plunges 215 feet past rocky cliffs that stand 400 feet over the gorge below. The park has several rim and gorge trails, offering views from both above and below the falls. Visitors are strongly advised to stay on the trails and not enter the water. The Gorge Trail is rated easy and open year round. The South Rim and North Rim trails are rated moderate and only open April through October.

Campsites and cabins are available overlooking Cayuga Lake. Nearby, there is a marina with a boat launch and a beach. However, the boat launch is not suitable for any kind of sailboat.

Best Time to Visit: The best time to visit Taughannock Falls State Park is during the spring for the flowing waterfalls and the fall for the vibrant foliage.

Pass/Permit/Fees: Admission is $9 for cars, $35 for noncommercial buses, $75 for commercial buses, or $75 for a seasonal bus pass.

Closest City or Town: Ithaca

Physical Address:
Taughannock Falls State Park
1740 Taughannock Boulevard
Trumansburg, NY 14886

GPS Coordinates: 42.54836° N, 76.60634° W

Did You Know? Taughannock Falls is the highest straight-drop waterfall this side of the Rocky Mountains.

The Finger Lakes

The Finger Lakes—Cayuga, Seneca, Canandaigua, Canadice, Conesus, Owasco, Keuka, Hemlock, Honeoye, Otisco, and Skaneateles—were carved from stream valleys by receding glaciers.

Visitors will find over 100 wineries, amazing restaurants, unique museums, art galleries, outdoor recreation, and dozens of waterfalls nearby. This area is the largest and most acclaimed winemaking region in the eastern U.S. While the local vineyards produce many varieties of wines, the cool-climate grape, the Riesling, has become the signature wine of the Finger Lakes, known the world over.

Best Time to Visit: The best time to visit the Finger Lakes is from May to September.

Pass/Permit/Fees: There are no fees to visit, but each activity will have fees associated with it.

Closest City or Town: Ithaca

Physical Address:
Finger Lake National Forest
4490 Picnic Area Road
Burdett, NY 14818

GPS Coordinates: 42.48956° N, 76.81373° W

Did You Know? The region is home to some of the world's most famous sparkling-wine productions outside of France's Champagne region.

Watkins Glen

Watkins Glen is one of the most well-known of the state parks in the Finger Lakes Region. Within the first 2 miles, the glen's stream makes a descent of 400 feet and passes 200-foot cliffs. Along its course, it creates 19 waterfalls.

The gorge's path travels over and under the waterfalls, and the park has several trails that afford a view of the gorge. A 2-mile hike will take visitors past the 19 waterfalls and up over 800 stairs. In addition to the Gorge Trail, there are several smaller branching trails.

Campers and visitors have access to an Olympic-sized pool. There are also picnic areas, fishing at Seneca Lake or Catherine Creek, and summer tours through the glen.

Best Time to Visit: The best time to visit Watkins Glen is mid-May to early June or September through late October.

Pass/Permit/Fees: Admission is $10 for cars, $35 for noncommercial buses, $75 for commercial buses, or $75 for a nonprofit seasonal bus pass.

Closest City or Town: Ithaca

Physical Address:
Watkins Glen State Park
1009 N. Franklin Street
Watkins Glen, NY 14891

GPS Coordinates: 42.46689° N, 76.88393° W

Did You Know? In 2015, the park was named one of the top three state parks in the country based on a national poll.

Crane Mountain

Crane Mountain is part of the Central Adirondacks, located in the Wilcox Lake Wild Forest. The mountain is 3,524 feet tall and has over 5 miles of hiking trails. While climbing, visitors will gain over 1,300 feet in elevation. Because there are some steep sections, this hike can be tough. There are two options to hike this mountain. Climbers can go straight to the summit via a 1.4-mile hike or take a 3-mile loop.

The lookouts around the summit offer visitors several great options for scenic views. In addition, there is a pond on the mountain's shoulder that is popular with fishermen. In the spring, visitors need to exercise caution in the areas around and leading up to the pond since they will be covered in ice.

Best Time to Visit: The best time to visit Crane Mountain is June through October.

Pass/Permit/Fees: There are no fees to visit this location.

Closest City or Town: Johnsburg

Physical Address:
Crane Mountain Trailhead
NY-8
Johnsburg, NY 12843

GPS Coordinates: 43.54356° N, 73.96816° W

Did You Know? Hikers do not have to climb the steep ladder to reach the summit and can go the long way instead.

Natural Stone Bridge & Caves

The Natural Stone Bridge & Caves offers visitors multiple options for exploring. During the self-guided, 20-stop tour, visitors will embark on a journey to see each cave. Sites include potholes, natural pools, and a brook that flows through a cavern. Alternatively, there is an Adventure Tour that allows visitors to wear a caving suit and actually go spelunking through the caves. For children, the site offers the option to dig for dinosaur bones, find treasure, uncover crystals, and play golf. For those who enjoy hiking, there are also two trails included with the admission fee. Visitors are required to book their tickets a day in advance.

Best Time to Visit: The best time to visit Natural Stone Bridge & Caves is in the summer and early winter since this is a seasonal location.

Pass/Permit/Fees: Self-guided tours are $18 for adults or $8.95 for children. Adventure tours are $125 and limited to adults only. Snowshoe trail access is $14.95 for adults and $8.50 for children with snowshoe rental available for $5.

Closest City or Town: Johnsburg

Physical Address:
Natural Stone Bridge & Caves
535 Stone Bridge Road
Pottersville, NY 12860

GPS Coordinates: 43.74821° N, 73.85198° W

Did You Know? This location features the largest cave entrance in the eastern United States, which is still being carved out by Trout Brook.

Avalanche Lake

Avalanche Lake is located in the Adirondacks High Peak Wilderness. Hiking in the high peaks can be difficult, with footpaths that seem to go directly up the mountain. Once visitors are near Avalanche Lake, the terrain will start to level out. However, there will still be large boulders they will have to navigate. The ADK club installed wooden ladders and catwalks around the trail. This not only makes the trail less challenging but also more fun.

There are still areas of the trail that will be overgrown. Hikers will have to pay attention to trail markers and their maps to ensure they do not get lost. Additionally, the area is rampant with black bears. Hikers will need to have bear cannisters available for storing their food.

Best Time to Visit: The best time to visit Avalanche Lake is May through October.

Pass/Permit/Fees: There is no fee for visiting this location.

Closest City or Town: Keene

Physical Address:
Avalanche Lake
Keene Valley, NY 12943

GPS Coordinates: 44.13157° N, 73.96950° W

Did You Know? The trail around the lake is 10.2 miles long and takes around 5 hours to complete.

Lake Placid

Located in the heart of the Adirondack Mountains, Lake Placid offers a variety of activities for visitors. Mirror Lake features a 2.7-mile walking path around the entire circumference. It has a beach at one end that serves as the start of the swimming portion of the Ironman Triathlon.

Once it freezes over, the lake becomes a skating rink for the whole town. The town also has its own mountain, Mount Jo, which is 2,876 feet tall. It features two trails to the summit. One is shorter and steeper, while the other is considered easy. ADK Aquatics offers wakeboarding, waterskiing, tubing, and wakesurfing, so there's something for everyone with training available from their expert staff. Visitors can also participate in scenic flights, bobsledding, and cross-country skiing.

Best Time to Visit: Lake Placid is open all year.

Pass/Permit/Fees: Fees vary per activity, but there is no entrance fee.

Closest City or Town: Keene

Physical Address:
Lake Placid World War 1 Memorial
31 Parkside Drive
Lake Placid, NY 12946

GPS Coordinates: 44.28614° N, 73.98338° W

Did You Know? Lake Placid was the site of the Winter Olympics in 1932 and 1980.

Ausable Chasm

Established in 1870, the Ausable Chasm is the oldest
natural attraction in the United States. The chasm is formed
from 500-million-year-old sandstone that dates back to the
Cambrian Period. It features over 5 miles of scenic trails
that visitors can hike, and the Ausable River can be toured
by floating on a tube or raft. The sandstone walls are even
climbable. Famous sites in the area include Rainbow Falls,
Elephants Head, and the Grand Flume. Activities include
float tours, nighttime lantern tours, the Adventure Trail,
rappelling, and rock climbing during the summer. These
activities are also offered during the spring and fall;
however, there may be some service limitations. During
winter, guests can take part in snowshoe and ice-cleat tours.

Best Time to Visit: The best time to visit Ausable Chasm
is September through October.

Pass/Permit/Fees: Admission is $17.95 for adults and
teenagers, $10 for local residents, $9.95 for children over
age 5, and free for children under 5. Tours will have
additional fees.

Closest City or Town: Keeseville

Physical Address:
Ausable Chasm
2144 U.S. 9
Ausable Chasm, NY 12911

GPS Coordinates: 44.53731° N, 73.46133° W

Did You Know? The chasm was flooded twice in 1996
with massive devastation to the bridges.

Bethel Woods Museum

The Bethel Woods Museum is located at the actual historic site of the 1969 Woodstock festival. The museum's purpose is to encourage a dialogue between generations about important ideas and issues that are still relevant. It explores the significance of the Woodstock festival as the culmination of a decade of transformation. The museum offers personal stories, musical and multi-media displays, and educational programs and events. It intends to inspire a new generation to effect positive change in the world around them. The museum is also actively involved in the surrounding community, offering education, economic development, and historic preservation.

Best Time to Visit: The best time to visit Bethel Woods Museum is April through December.

Pass/Permit/Fees: Online/in-person tickets are $17/$19.69 for adults, $15/$17 for seniors, $5/$7 for children over age 5, and free for children under 5. Admission to the special exhibit only is $5 for all ages.

Closest City or Town: Liberty

Physical Address:
Bethel Woods Museum
200 Hurd Road
Bethel, NY 12720

GPS Coordinates: 41.71095° N, 74.87675° W

Did You Know? The museum has more artifacts in secure storage than they do on display.

Montauk Point

Montauk Point State Park is located on the eastern tip of the South Shore of Long Island. It offers a unique view of the convergence of the Atlantic Ocean and the Block Island Sound. During times when the water is calm, visitors can see the race of the converging tides from the two bodies of water. There are nature trails available for hiking in the warmer months and cross-country skiing in the winter months. Visitors can also watch the seals sunning themselves on the rocks at the shore. The Montauk Point Lighthouse is a National Maritime Historic Landmark located 50 feet from the edge of the bluff, and it's constantly threatened by erosion. Efforts to restore the bluff and preserve the lighthouse have already reached $1 million.

Best Time to Visit: Visit in October through November.

Pass/Permit/Fees: Admission is $8 for cars, $35 for nonprofit buses, and $75 for corporate buses. Visiting the lighthouse is an additional cost.

Closest City or Town: Long Island

Physical Address:
Montauk Lighthouse Museum
2000 Montauk Highway
Montauk, NY 11954

GPS Coordinates: 41.09508° N, 71.85864° W

Did You Know? The original construction of the lighthouse was completed in 1796 at the direction of President Washington.

Bannerman Castle

Bannerman Castle is a fairytale-like structure with a truly banal backstory. It was built as a storage facility for a New York City–based military-surplus business. Those approaching from the north end can still view the words *Bannerman's Island Arsenal* on the wall. Born in 1851 in Northern Ireland, Francis Bannerman VI emigrated to the U.S. with his parents in 1854. His family settled near the Brooklyn Navy Yard. In his teens, he began a business dealing with military-surplus supplies.

At the end of the Spanish-American War, Bannerman purchased 90 percent of the Spanish arms. Needing a place to store all of it, he purchased Pollepel Island in 1900 and designed his storehouse to look like the castles of Scotland.

Best Time to Visit: The best time to visit Bannerman's Castle is May through October.

Pass/Permit/Fees: Admission is $37.50 for adults and $32.50 for children.

Closest City or Town: Newburgh

Physical Address:
Bannerman Castle
Pollepel Island
Beacon, NY 12508

GPS Coordinates: 41.45544° N, 73.98878° W

Did You Know? Pollepel Island was uninhabited for most of its history because the Native Americans considered it to be haunted.

36

Breakneck Ridge

Breakneck Ridge is a mountain located between Beacon and Cold Spring. It is well-known for its rocky trails and excellent views of the Hudson River. Considered one of the most difficult hikes in New York, it's easily accessible and extremely popular. Large portions of the hike require climbers to lift themselves over large rocks using both their hands and feet. This allows them to gain elevation very quickly.

There are three trail options. The shorter Breakneck Ridge loop should take hikers around 2 hours to complete. The full classic loop, on the other hand, will take about 3 hours. The Breakneck to Cold Spring trail is the longest and will take hikers 4 to 5 hours to complete. All times will be dependent on the number of stops hikers take along the trails.

Best Time to Visit: The best time to visit Breakneck Ridge is during the fall to see the foliage.

Pass/Permit/Fees: There is no cost to hike these trails.

Closest City or Town: Newburgh

Physical Address:
Breakneck Ridge Trailhead
472 Bear Mountain-Beacon Highway
Cold Spring, NY 10516

GPS Coordinates: 41.44382°N, 73.97817° W

Did You Know? The tallest summit is roughly 1,260 feet above sea level.

Sam's Point Preserve

Located in the highest part of the Shawangunk Mountains, Sam's Point Preserve is the southernmost section of the Minnewaska State Park Preserve. It's comprised of roughly 5,000 acres that includes a forest of pitch pine surrounded by chestnut oaks.

Sam's Point Preserve is the home of Lake Maratanza, which is one of Shawangunk's five sky lakes. It also has ice-cave crevices that visitors can explore. One of its scenic vistas is a 187-foot waterfall called Verkeerder Kill Falls, which is located on private property. Visitors should note that the preserve has a very small parking area. In order to obtain entry, visitors will need to arrive early or visit during nonpeak times.

Best Time to Visit: The best time to visit Sam's Point Preserve is during spring and summer.

Pass/Permit/Fees: Admission is $10 for cars, $60 for nonprofit bus passes, and $100 for commercial bus passes.

Closest City or Town: Newburgh

Physical Address:
Sam's Point Area of Minnewaska State Park Preserve
400 Sam's Point Road
Cragsmoor, NY 12420

GPS Coordinates: 41.67107° N, 74.36177° W

Did You Know? The name Sam's Point comes from a legend of a man named Sam who leaped to his death from the point while being chased by Native Americans.

5 Beekman Street

5 Beekman Street is located one block from City Hall. Sitting empty in the decade leading up to 2016, parts of it had been shuttered as early as the 1940s. It was the third building in the city to have an elevator, and the building features a full-height atrium and skylight.

Constructed in 1882, it was originally built to house a theater. Shakespeare's *Hamlet* premiered in the theater, making it the first time the play was shown to an American audience and the theater's first historical event.

Now, the building houses a luxury hotel that features all of the classical architecture it was known for.

Best Time to Visit: 5 Beekman Street is open all year.

Pass/Permit/Fees: There is no fee to visit.

Closest City or Town: New York City

Physical Address:
5 Beekman Street
New York, NY 10038

GPS Coordinates: 40.71215° N, 74.00687° W

Did You Know? The building received historical status in 1998.

9/11 Memorial and Museum

The 9/11 Memorial and Museum is located at the site of the former Twin Towers as a memorial to remember the lives of those lost in the attacks on September 11, 2001, and February 26, 1993. The names of the victims are inscribed on bronze bulwarks on the reflecting pools, arranged according to an algorithm that creates a meaningful lineup. The museum itself is built underground with its entrance located in close proximity to the monument. The memorial is a quiet place to reflect on the tragedies that took place.

Best Time to Visit: The museum is open Thursday through Monday from 10 a.m. to 5 p.m. The memorial is open daily during the same hours.

Pass/Permit/Fees: Museum admission prices are $26 for adults, $7 for children ages 7–12, $20 for children ages 13–17, $20 for college students, and $18 for veterans. The memorial is free.

Closest City or Town: New York City

Physical Address:
9/11 Memorial and Museum
180 Greenwich Street
New York, NY 10007

GPS Coordinates: 40.71028° N, 74.01229° W

Did You Know? The museum also holds information and exhibits related to the February 26, 1993, terrorist bombing of the World Trade Center.

6 1/2 Avenue: Manhattan's Secret Street

Given its official signposts in July 2012 by the Department of Transportation, 6 ½ Avenue is the only street in New York City with a fractional number. This secret avenue is located in the public spaces between 57th and 51st streets. Midtown workers are already long familiar with the avenue and use it to avoid walking around to 6th or 7th Avenue.

The DOT added high-visibility crosswalks, reflective markers, and stop signs on cross streets along 6 ½ Avenue to assist pedestrians with making their way safely down the street. The avenue cuts through open-access lobbies, which are also known as privately owned public spaces, or POPS. Local business owners are responsible for maintaining their POPS.

Best Time to Visit: 6 ½ Avenue is open all year.

Pass/Permit/Fees: There is no fee associated with this location.

Closest City or Town: New York City

Physical Address:
6 ½ Avenue
51st Street
New York, NY 10022

GPS Coordinates: 40.76394° N, 73.98034° W

Did You Know? The mid-block stop signs are unusual for Manhattan and lead to traffic problems.

African Burial Ground National Monument

In 1991, when construction for the Ted Weiss Federal Building at 190 Broadway began, a burial site for 15,000 free and enslaved Africans was discovered just below the surface of the street. The skeletal remains dated back from the mid-1630s to 1795. It is the largest cemetery for people of African descent from the Colonial Era. In 1993, the site was named a National Historic Landmark. Then, in 2006, President George W. Bush designated it a National Monument. The mission of the African Burial Ground National Monument is to promote understanding, continue research, and present educational opportunities visitors better understand and honor the culture and contributions of Africans and Americans of African descent.

Best Time to Visit: Visit the African Burial Ground National Monument Tuesday through Saturday.

Pass/Permit/Fees: Entry is free of charge.

Closest City or Town: New York City

Physical Address:
African Burial Ground National Monument
290 Broadway
New York, NY 10007

GPS Coordinates: 40.71538° N, 74.00447° W

Did You Know? The African Burial Ground was created because New York's African population was only allowed to be buried in desolate and unappropriated land.

Alice in Wonderland Statue

The Alice in Wonderland Statue is located in Central Park just north of the Conservatory Water at East 74th Street. The statute stands 11 feet tall and is made of bronze. It features Alice and her cat seated on a mushroom with the Mad Hatter, the Cheshire Cat, the White Rabbit, and the Dormouse surrounding her.

Philanthropist George Delacorte commissioned the piece, and artist Jose de Creeft constructed it in 1959. It was intended as a gift to the children of the city so that they could visit and experience the classic story. Unlike most sculptures, children are invited to climb, touch, and crawl all over this one. The design was created based on the original illustrations from the first edition of the book. Alice's face was modeled after Creeft's daughter Donna.

Best Time to Visit: The Alice in Wonderland Statue is open all year.

Pass/Permit/Fees: There is no fee to visit this location.

Closest City or Town: New York City

Physical Address:
Alice in Wonderland
E. 74th Street
New York, NY 10021

GPS Coordinates: 40.77585° N, 73.96663° W

Did You Know? The Mad Hatter is a caricature of George Delacorte.

Broadway Flea Market

The Broadway Flea Market is a 1-day event that occurs every year in September. This flea market and auction stretches from Shubert Alley into Times Square, filling West 44th Street. The flea market features tables of wares, silent auctions, live auctions, and even private video chats with Broadway stars. All of the money donated at the Broadway Flea Market goes toward providing medication, healthcare, meals, and emergency support for those living with HIV/AIDS, COVID-19, or other life-threatening illnesses. Their efforts support all 50 states, Puerto Rico, and Washington, D.C. The flea market debuted in 1987, raising $12,000. Since then, a total of 35 events have been held with a collective total of $16.5 million raised.

Best Time to Visit: Visit the Broadway Flea Market in September.

Pass/Permit/Fees: There is no fee to visit this location.

Closest City or Town: New York City

Physical Address:
Broadway Flea Market
Shubert Alley
New York, NY 10036

GPS Coordinates: 40.75817° N, 73.98695° W

Did You Know? The Broadway Flea Market is run by Broadway Cares/Equity Fights AIDS, who has raised over $300 million for necessary services for those living with chronic conditions across a variety of fundraisers and events.

Broadway Theatre

The Broadway Theatre contains 1,761 seats. Unlike most of the other Broadway theatres, this one is actually located on Broadway. Originally, it opened as a film house called B. S. Moss's Colony. In modern times, the theatre features plays and musicals like *Aladdin*, *Beetlejuice*, *Birthday Candles*, *The Book of Mormon*, *Hangtown*, *Hamilton*, *The Little Prince*, and *The Lion King*. Tickets for the most popular shows tend to sell out months in advance, so visitors are encouraged to plan accordingly.

Best Time to Visit: The best time to visit is January and February when it is easier and cheaper to get seats.

Pass/Permit/Fees: Fees vary by show, date, and seat selection.

Closest City or Town: New York City

Physical Address:
Broadway Theatre
1681 Broadway
New York, NY 10019

GPS Coordinates: 40.76324° N, 73.98313° W

Did You Know? There are 41 total theatres under the Broadway umbrella in New York City.

Bryant Park Bathrooms

The Bryant Park bathrooms are likely the most luxurious public bathrooms in all of New York City. They boast fresh flowers, artwork, and a classical-music soundtrack. Located in the Beaux Arts Building, these restrooms are funded by private donors. They offer two stalls for men and three for women. Light is allowed to gently spill into the space through large, frosted-glass windows

The building is a historic landmark and underwent a $300,000 renovation in 2017. New Toto toilets, fresh tiles, and a modern air-conditioning system were all added. Bathroom attendants do not accept tips. The restrooms are wheelchair accessible.

Best Time to Visit: Bryant Park bathrooms are open all year.

Pass/Permit/Fees: There is no fee to visit this location.

Closest City or Town: New York City

Physical Address:
Bryant Park
W. 42nd Street
New York, NY 10018

GPS Coordinates: 40.75454° N, 73.98241° W

Did You Know? The toilets, sinks, and other fixtures are the same luxury brand used at the Museum of Modern Art.

Chinatown

There are several things to do in Chinatown. First, visitors can learn about Chinese-American history and culture at the Museum of Chinese in America. Next, a trip down Mott Street will capture the experience of everything Chinatown has to offer. There is a food tour available where a chef takes visitors on a tour of the restaurants available in the neighborhood. Magic Jewelry NYC offers aura readings, and guests can also buy a variety of jewelry, including, necklaces, bracelets, and earrings. At Meow Parlour, visitors can stop in for some coffee and playtime with the owner's five cats. The Canal Street Market offers the experience of a real market where visitors can haggle for the best prices possible. Columbus Park offers a place where locals gather for communal exercise.

Best Time to Visit: Visit before 6 p.m. any day of the week. However, it's best to avoid the neighborhood on Sunday since trash does not get picked up until Monday.

Pass/Permit/Fees: There are no fees except for tours.

Closest City or Town: New York City

Physical Address:
Chinatown Information Kiosk
Baxter and Canal Street
New York, NY 10013

GPS Coordinates: 40.71575° N, 73.99703° W

Did You Know? Chinatown was originally created in the late 1800s as a safe haven for Chinese immigrants who were driven out of the West by an anti-Chinese movement.

City Hall Station

On October 27, 1904, the first subway station in New York City opened beneath City Hall. The station was designed with many fine architectural details, including glass tiles, immense skylights, and glass chandeliers. However, it was rife with problems from the start. As it was designed with a curved platform, central doors on the trains could not be used at this station unless they were specifically modified for the platform. This meant that only the end doors could be used. In 1945, the station temporarily closed due to modifications on platforms along the line. For many riders, getting to destinations in Brooklyn was easier by walking on the street level to the Brooklyn Bridge Station.

Best Time to Visit: It's best to visit on days that are bright and sunny so that the station is naturally lit up by the skylights.

Pass/Permit/Fees: Tour tickets are $50, and membership to the museum is $60.

Closest City or Town: New York City

Physical Address:
City Hall Station
Broadway
New York, NY 10007

GPS Coordinates: 40.71360° N, 74.00671° W

Did You Know? While the station is considered abandoned, the number 6 trains still use the tracks as a turnaround point roughly every 8 minutes.

Clock Tower Building

Construction on the Clock Tower Building was completed in 1894. It was originally the home of the New York Life Insurance Company until they moved to their Madison Square headquarters in 1927. The building was used to house other offices until 1967 when it was purchased by New York City to house several municipal offices. By the 1970s, however, it sat largely abandoned, and the clock was in a state of disrepair. In 1972, the space right below the clock was established as the Clocktower Gallery. This brought artists into close contact with the clock, and some of them incorporated it into their work. Municipal workers repaired the clocktower later that decade. The tower is now an apartment complex and not open to the public on the inside. However, visitors can walk down the street to view the iconic structure at any time of day.

Best Time to Visit: Visitors can come to this location at any time of the year.

Pass/Permit/Fees: There is no fee associated with this location.

Closest City or Town: New York City

Physical Address:
Clock Tower Building
346 Broadway
New York, NY 10013

GPS Coordinates: 40.71952° N, 74.00405° W

Did You Know? Each minute hand of the clock weighs half a ton.

Crabs of Cleopatra's Needle

The crabs emerging underneath Cleopatra's Needle are replicas of the original crab-themed support structure created by the Romans thousands of years ago. Originally built as part of a pair in Egypt, this obelisk was sent to New York while its mate was sent to England. The pair, along with a third needle that now resides in Paris, are all commonly known as Cleopatra's Needle.

In February 1881, the New York Cleopatra's Needle was gifted to the United States by Egypt as a thank you for its neutrality in the middle of a situation between Egypt and the European powers. Once it arrived in the U.S., 32 horses were hitched together in pairs to haul the obelisk from the Hudson River to Central Park.

Best Time to Visit: It's best to visit during the summer and fall when there is no snow on the ground.

Pass/Permit/Fees: There is no fee associated with this location.

Closest City or Town: New York City

Physical Address:
Cleopatra's Needle
Metropolitan Museum of Art, Central Park West
New York, NY 10024

GPS Coordinates: 40.80446° N, 73.96518° W

Did You Know? It took 4 months to move Cleopatra's Needle from the Hudson River to its home in Central Park when it was first brought to New York.

Dream House

The Dream House was created in 1993 by a husband-and-wife team made up of composer La Monte Young and visual artist Marian Zazeela. This unique experience is located in an apartment on Church Street in Tribeca. The whole apartment is filled with neon pink that is paired with constantly pulsating sound waves. All moves that visitors make will be accompanied by a new collection of sounds and pitches. Sounds change based on whether visitors are sitting, standing, laying down, in the front of the apartment, or in the back of the apartment. It is intended to be a completely immersive experience for the viewer. Removal of shoes, bags, and jackets is required at the entrance. The owners do request that visitors maintain silence while in the Dream House. Although there is air conditioning, the venue can get quite stuffy. Additionally, it is not wheelchair accessible.

Best Time to Visit: The Dream House is open 2 p.m. to 2 a.m. Wednesday through Saturday.

Pass/Permit/Fees: Admission is $10.

Closest City or Town: New York City

Physical Address:
Dream House
275 Church Street
New York, NY 10013

GPS Coordinates: 40.71989° N, 74.00478° W

Did You Know? The Dream House is a nonprofit business that's maintained through donations.

Empire State Building

The purpose of creating the Empire State Building was to have a location to house offices and beat the record for the tallest building in the world. When it was constructed in 1931, this meant being taller than the Bank of Manhattan and the Chrysler Building. At 102 stories, the Empire State Building held the record until 1971. Its original height was 1,250 feet tall, with a little extra of that height coming from its spire on the top. It has a special LED lighting system that changes colors based on holidays and celebrations. This has been a tradition since 1976 when its first lighting system was installed. John Raskob and Al Smith were the designers behind the construction of the building.

Best Time to Visit: At 8 a.m., 3 p.m., and midnight, the crowds are thinnest, offering the best times to visit.

Pass/Permit/Fees: Main-deck admission is $44 for adults, $42 for seniors, and $38 for children. Top-deck admission is $77 for adults, $75 for seniors, and $71 for children.

Closest City or Town: New York City

Physical Address:
Empire State Building
20 W. 34th Street
New York, NY 10001

GPS Coordinates: 40.74795° N, 73.98572° W

Did You Know? The Empire State Building has undergone extreme green-architecture initiatives that reduced energy usage and emissions and increased efficiency.

Explorers Club Headquarters

The Explorers Club was founded in 1904 by Henry Collins Walsh and other Arctic explorers. They purchased the building in 1960, making it the official international headquarters in 1965. The various floors of the building house a century's worth of collected artifacts. Most impressively, the top floor holds the research archives. This floor contains 13,000 books; 5,000 maps; 1,000 museum objects; and 500 films. The gallery is also located on the top floor, and it houses a variety of taxidermized specimens. Club members focus on climate change and animal and human preservation. Membership is restricted to those that have proven themselves in the field of exploration.

Best Time to Visit: The headquarters are open 9 a.m. to 6 p.m. Monday through Friday and during special events. Visitors are welcome during open hours.

Pass/Permit/Fees: Fees are based on the events attended.

Closest City or Town: New York City

Physical Address:
Explorers Club
46 E. 70th Street
New York, NY 10021

GPS Coordinates: 40.77089° N, 73.96568° W

Did You Know? The ceiling of the Explorers Club Headquarters was purchased from a 15th-century Italian monastery, and the windows are originals from Windsor Castle, featuring stained glass inlaid with Tudor Roses.

Fearless Girl Statue

Erected on March 7, 2017, the *Fearless Girl* statue has been the subject of controversy. Many critics view it as fake corporate feminism. Additionally, the company that commissioned the piece, State Street, filed a lawsuit in February 2019 against the artist for selling replicas of the statue in several countries. The statue features a young girl standing determinedly with her hands on her hips. She currently stands facing down Wall Street, but her original position was facing the *Charging Bull* statue.

Best Time to Visit: As the statue is on public property, visitors can view it all day, year round.

Pass/Permit/Fees: There are no fees associated with this location.

Closest City or Town: New York City

Physical Address:
Fearless Girl Statue
Broad Street
New York, NY 10004

GPS Coordinates: 40.70647° N, 74.01336° W

Did You Know? In September 2017, State Street, the company that commissioned the statue, agreed to pay $5 million following claims by the U.S. Department of Labor that the company had discriminated against Black and female employees through their pay practices.

Graffiti Hall of Fame

Established in 1980 by Harlem Community leader Ray Rodriguez in the schoolyard of the Jackie Robinson Educational Complex, the Graffiti Hall of Fame was created for up-and-coming graffiti artists to work on their craft in a safe space. Originally, Rodriguez and his supporters intended it as a space for graffiti artists to practice their skills during the time the art was moving from simple tags to complex wall murals. All four of the schoolyard's walls are fair game for artwork. Today, it's geared more toward professionals with amateurs no longer creating their art here. A rotation of world-renowned street artists visits the Graffiti Hall of Fame to leave a piece of art. Because of the attention it has brought to the school complex, the yard has undergone a renovation, making it as clean and presentable as the artwork on its walls.

Best Time to Visit: The best time to visit is on weekends and other times when school is not in session.

Pass/Permit/Fees: There is no fee associated with this location.

Closest City or Town: New York City

Physical Address:
Graffiti Hall of Fame
Park Avenue
New York, NY 10029

GPS Coordinates: 40.79431° N, 73.94798° W

Did You Know? The school complex threatens to arrest unauthorized visitors while the school is open.

Grand Central Terminal Whispering Gallery

A special in Grand Central Terminal allows two people to stand at opposite sides, speak in regular voices, and perfectly hear each other. The Grand Central Terminal Whispering Gallery is made possible by the unusually perfect arches.

The space is located on the lower concourse outside the Oyster Bar restaurant. As this location can be very busy, visitors will need to plan on coming when it is not a peak commuting time. Too much noise will disturb the effect of the noise transmission across the gallery.

Best Time to Visit: The best time to visit is during nonpeak hours so that this acoustic anomaly can be optimally experienced.

Pass/Permit/Fees: There is no fee associated with this location.

Closest City or Town: New York City

Physical Address:
Whispering Gallery in Grand Central Terminal
89 E. 42nd Street
New York, NY 10017

GPS Coordinates: 40.75334° N< 73.97730° W

Did You Know? The distinctive tiles that make up the gallery are known as "Gustavino tiles," named for Spanish tile maker Rafael Gustavino.

Greenacre Park

A 60-foot by 120-foot vest-pocket park, Greenacre Park is an urban open space that features a 25-foot waterfall running over sculpted rocks. The park is open to the sky with a centralized area that features 12 mature honey locust trees and a café. It is comprised of three levels. There is also a covered terrace area that contains heating elements to warm visitors during the cooler months. The park is privately owned and maintained by the Greenacre Foundation. If the staff feel that an activity disrupts the serenity of the park, then it will not be allowed. For instance, smoking, alcoholic beverages, commercial photography, private events, pets, bicycles, skateboards, scooters, musical instruments, and other audio sources are all prohibited in the park.

Best Time to Visit: The park is open from April through December and is best visited in the fall when the foliage is bright.

Pass/Permit/Fees: There are no fees associated with this location.

Closest City or Town: New York City

Physical Address:
Greenacre Park
217 E. 51st Street
New York, NY 10022

GPS Coordinates: 40.75663° N, 73.96931° W

Did You Know? Greenacre Park is on the National Register of Historic Places.

Hess Triangle

In 1910, while 300 buildings were demolished to expand the streets and construct new subway lines, one man fought to keep his building. David Hess battled the city to maintain ownership of his apartment building, the Voorhis. He eventually lost, and by 1914, all that was left was a 500-square-inch triangle.

When asked to donate this piece to the city sidewalk, Hess refused out of spite. On July 27, 1922, he covered the triangle with mosaic tiles and the words *Property of the Hess Estate Which Has Never Been Dedicated For Public Purposes.*

The triangle is currently located outside of a cigar shop on the corner of Christopher Street and 7th Avenue.

Best Time to Visit: Visit during months without snow so that the ground will be clear to view the triangle.

Pass/Permit/Fees: There is no fee associated with this location.

Closest City or Town: New York City

Physical Address:
Hess Triangle
110 7th Avenue South
New York, NY 10014

GPS Coordinates: 40.73430° N, 74.00307° W

Did You Know? Village Cigars purchased the triangle in 1938 for $1,000.

High Bridge

The Old Croton Aqueduct went into service in 1842 but could not provide enough water to the city on its own. In 1848, the High Bridge opened, bringing water from the Croton River to Manhattan by way of two pipes. In the early 1860s, the two pipes were replaced by a single one. Between 1927 and 1928, the five arches were replaced by the single arch that remains today. Protests to protect the bridge outweighed the movement to remove it. The bridge now has designation as a New York City landmark, and because it is part of the Old Croton Aqueduct, it shares the aqueduct's designation as a National Historic Landmark. The bridge was closed for 45 years and reopened in 2015 following an extensive restoration. It is now accessible to everyone, including people in wheelchairs.

Best Time to Visit: The bridge is accessible year round from 7 a.m. to 8 p.m.

Pass/Permit/Fees: There are no fees associated with this location.

Closest City or Town: New York City

Physical Address:
The High Bridge
Harlem River Drive
New York, NY 10033

GPS Coordinates: 40.84307° N, 73.93019° W

Did You Know? At both ends of the bridge, there are attic spaces connected by catwalks where visitors can see the remains of the old aqueduct system.

Holographic Studios Inc.

Located in the heart of NYC, Holographic Studios operates the world's oldest gallery of holography. They even have a subterranean laser laboratory where they create their own holograms. They offer hands-on classes on holography and a lecture series led by owner Jason Sapan. He has experience teaching holography at NYU and is well-suited to explaining the subject. Additionally, he has used his laser skills to create photography, laser shows, and art installations.

Best Time to Visit: The gallery is open Monday through Friday from 2 p.m. to 6 p.m. by appointment only.

Pass/Permit/Fees: Tours are $35 per person. On weekends, there is an additional $35 fee per group, and groups can pay $100 on top of that to make their tour a private one. For $150 per person, visitors can create a hologram during their tour.

Closest City or Town: New York City

Physical Address:
Holographic Studios
240 E. 26th Street
New York, NY 10010

GPS Coordinates: 40.74063° N, 73.98017° W

Did You Know? Holographic Studios's founder has been creating and teaching about holography since the 1960s.

Intrepid Sea, Air, & Space Museum

The Intrepid Sea, Air, & Space Museum is focused on history, science, and service. The museum was founded in 1982. It features the historic aircraft carrier *The Intrepid*, which is a National Historic Landmark. This carrier is the survivor of five kamikaze strikes and one torpedo strike. It served tours in both Vietnam and World War II before it was decommissioned in 1974. There are also 28 aircraft that include the world's fastest military jet. Visitors can enter *Growler*, the only guided-missile submarine that is open to the public. Other highlights include the space shuttle *Enterprise* and the *Concorde*. Visitors of every age are taken on an interactive adventure.

Best Time to Visit: The museum is open Monday through Sunday from 10 a.m. to 5 p.m. all year except for Christmas and Thanksgiving.

Pass/Permit/Fees: Admission is $33 for guests ages 13–64, $31 for seniors over age 64, $24 for children ages 5–12, and free for children under 5.

Closest City or Town: New York City

Physical Address:
Intrepid Sea, Air & Space Museum
Pier 86
New York, NY 10036

GPS Coordinates: 40.76531° N, 73.99956° W

Did You Know? The museum holds many activities and programs related to STEM learning each year.

Strawberry Fields John Lennon Memorial

Strawberry Fields is adjacent to the Dakota Apartments where John Lennon lived with his wife Yoko Ono. The actual location of the memorial is on their favorite spot in Central Park. The space is lined with elm trees, shrubs, flowers, and rocks. Strawberry Fields is designated as a quiet zone in Central Park. The central part of the memorial is a mosaic that has *Imagine* in the center of it. In 1984, Yoko Ono contributed $500,000 for a remodel of the memorial and an equivalent amount for an endowment to cover ongoing maintenance.

Best Time to Visit: The most popular times to visit are October 9 on John Lennon's birthday and December 8 on the anniversary of his murder. Visiting in the fall is great for the bright foliage, and the spring is the perfect time to see the blooming flowers.

Pass/Permit/Fees: There are no fees associated with this location.

Closest City or Town: New York City

Physical Address:
Strawberry Fields John Lennon Memorial
W. 72nd Street
New York, NY 10019

GPS Coordinates: 40.77619° N, 73.97479° W

Did You Know? The memorial is named for The Beatles song "Strawberry Fields Forever."

Long Lines Building

The Long Lines Building is a windowless skyscraper in the middle of Manhattan that was designed in 1974. While it is most well-known for its absolute lack of windows, it also has unusually high ceilings and can bear an extreme amount of weight per square foot. It was originally created to hold AT&T's carrier exchanges for long-distance switches and equipment. Today, it still does this but also stores a portion of the company's data-center processing.

In more recent times, there are reports that the Long Lines Building is housing NSA spying equipment for government data collection and wiretapping under code name TITANPOINTE.

Best Time to Visit: Visitors can view the exterior of the building all day, year round. Public entry is not permitted.

Pass/Permit/Fees: There is no fee associated with this location.

Closest City or Town: New York City

Physical Address:
AT&T Long Lines Building
211-227 Worth Street
New York, NY 10013

GPS Coordinates: 40.71449° N, 73.99866° W

Did You Know? The building can survive a nuclear fallout and can function off grid for up to two weeks with no problems.

Metropolitan Museum of Art

The Metropolitan Museum of Art was founded in 1870 and opened in its current Central Park location in 1880. The exhibits span over 5,000 years of history include more than 3,000,000 artifacts, although not all of them can be displayed at once. The Modern Art section features mostly American paintings along with a smaller collection of 19th-century European paintings. The American wing has the country's best collection of paintings, sculptures, and decorative arts. In the medieval section, visitors will find art from the 4th through 16th centuries. Tours are available in multiple languages. Many movies, including *When Harry Met Sally* and *The Thomas Crown Affair,* have shown this iconic location.

Best Time to Visit: The museum is open Thursday through Tuesday from 10 a.m. to 5 p.m.

Pass/Permit/Fees: Admission is $25 for adults, $17 for seniors, and $12 for students. Members, patrons, and children under the age of 12 may visit for free.

Closest City or Town: New York City

Physical Address:
Metropolitan Museum of Art
1000 5th Avenue
New York, NY 10028

GPS Coordinates: 40.77936° N, 73.96328° W

Did You Know? On a weekly basis, Remcoe van Vliet creates five towering bouquets of flowers for the entrance to the Met. These bouquets can reach up to 12 feet high.

Mmuseumm

Mmuseumm is a curated display of artifacts held in a freight elevator. It features both permanent and rotating collections, and the museum only fits three people at a time. Visitors are offered the opportunity to engage with both familiar and exotic objects from around the world. Mmuseumm was created by filmmakers Alex Kalman, Benny Safdie, and Josh Safdie. It was sponsored by the fashion industry's Kate Spade. The shoe that was thrown at President George W. Bush in Baghdad and a plastic glove from Paradise Valley, Montana, are among the unusual objects that have been displayed at this museum. The collection is changed and refreshed annually. It also has a small gift shop one window down that was added in 2018.

Best Time to Visit: Mmuseumm is open Friday through Sunday from 11 a.m. to 6 p.m. It's closed December through March.

Pass/Permit/Fees: $5 is the suggested donation for visitors.

Closest City or Town: New York City

Physical Address:
Mmuseumm
4 Cortlandt Alley
New York, NY 10013

GPS Coordinates: 40.71819° N, 74.00280° W

Did You Know? The museum is accessible 24 hours a day through a peephole in its door.

Museum of Reclaimed Urban Space

The goal of the Museum of Reclaimed Urban Space is to protect and tell the story of its archives. They also promote urban activism, research, and archival efforts to create community spaces. They put materials on exhibit that document these activities in order to educate visitors on the political undertones of reclaimed space. In the 1950s and 1960s, the wealthy began to move to the suburbs, causing property values to plummet. Landlords, seeing no point in paying taxes, collected rent until the city repossessed the buildings. Several neighborhoods were left abandoned in efforts known as planned shrinkage. In the late 1960s, struggling artists, punks, activists, and transients rebuilt the abandoned properties. In the 1980s, people began to move back into the city because of this group's work.

Best Time to Visit: Visit the museum on Tuesday or Thursday through Sunday from 1 p.m. to 6 p.m.

Pass/Permit/Fees: $5 is the suggested donation for visitors. Tours are $20.

Closest City or Town: New York City

Physical Address:
Museum of Reclaimed Urban Space (MoRUS)
155 Loisaida Avenue
New York, NY 10009

GPS Coordinates: 40.72655° N, 73.97782° W

Did You Know? Following Hurricane Sandy, many people were able to charge their phones using a battery-charging bicycle in the basement of MoRUS.

Mysterious Bookshop

Founded in 1979 by Otto Penzler, the Mysterious Bookshop is the world's biggest and oldest bookstore, dealing only in mystery, espionage, crime fiction, and thrillers. The store is located in Tribeca next to La Pain Quotidien and down the street from a 7-Eleven. The walls are covered all the way up to what seems like 20-foot ceilings with books in which someone likely dies a violent and untimely death. The store features copies of long-canceled detective magazines and a Sherlock Holmes section that includes all the spinoffs written by a variety of authors. There's even a section of mystery books involving mysterious books. The bookstore does not feature props, artwork, or pranks. It is a place of worship for the mystery genre.

Best Time to Visit: Visit the Mysterious Bookshop Monday through Saturday from 11 a.m. to 7 p.m.

Pass/Permit/Fees: There is no fee to visit this location, but there is a charge for purchasing books.

Closest City or Town: New York City

Physical Address:
Mysterious Book Shop
58 Warren Street
New York, NY 10007

GPS Coordinates: 40.71577° N, 74.009211° W

Did You Know? The bookstore's biblio-mystery series features some of the genre's biggest authors who write novellas exclusively for the store.

National Museum of Mathematics

The mission of the National Museum of Mathematics is to increase public understanding and perception of mathematics. It is well-known for its special tricycle that has square wheels yet runs smoothly on a catenary surface. The museum began in response to the closing of the Goudreau Museum on Long Island, which was dedicated to mathematics. A working group led by Glen Whitney met in August 2008 and discovered the lack of a mathematics museum in the U.S. despite demand. To date, their accomplishments include creation of the Math Midway exhibition, leading math tours in various U.S. cities, the *Math Encounters* series, and raising over $22 million.

Best Time to Visit: Visit the National Museum of Mathematics any day of the week between 10 a.m. and 5 p.m. except when it's closed for Thanksgiving Day.

Pass/Permit/Fees: Admission is $25 for adults, $20 for children 12 and under, $20 for students or seniors with ID, and free for members.

Closest City or Town: New York City

Physical Address:
National Museum of Mathematics
11 E. 26th Street
New York, NY 10010

GPS Coordinates: 40.74433° N, 73.98718° W

Did You Know? The National Museum of Mathematics is the only museum in North America that is dedicated to mathematics.

National Museum of the American Indian

Opened in October 1994, the National Museum of the American Indian is located in lower Manhattan in the Alexander Hamilton U.S. Custom House. The U.S. Custom House is considered to be an architectural jewel. It is located in New York's financial district and was completed in 1907. The museum features permanent and temporary exhibitions as well as public programs to explore the diversity of the Indigenous peoples of America. Music and dance performances, films, and symposia are all offered as part of the educational content. The *Infinity of Nations* exhibition audio tour is available in both English and Spanish, and there are Visitor Services volunteers who speak a variety of languages, including Spanish, Portuguese, Turkish, and Italian.

Best Time to Visit: Visit the museum from Monday through Friday during the hours of 10 a.m. to 5 p.m.

Pass/Permit/Fees: There are no fees.

Closest City or Town: New York City

Physical Address:
National Museum of the American Indian
1 Bowling Green
New York, NY 10004

GPS Coordinates: 40.70480° N, 74.01373° W

Did You Know? The museum is located on what was once the southern end of the Wiechquaekeck Trail.

Patent Pending

Patent Pending is a discreet cocktail bar located in the Radio Wave Building. In the daytime, the building's storefront café, Patent Coffee, serves its wares openly. At 5 p.m., the coffee shop becomes a front for a bar tucked behind the menu board. The walls, menu design, and lighting of the bar all reference Nikola Tesla. However, Patent Pending's craft drinks are unique creations of their own. They include such obscure ingredients as Tasmanian pepperberry, Szechuan peppercorn, and cardoon. Visitors are allowed in on a first come, first served basis.

In 2021, the owners opened another bar called The Lab inside of Patent Pending. It is available for corporate events and private parties.

Best Time to Visit: The best time to visit Patent Pending is between 5 p.m. and 2 a.m. daily. The last seating is 45 minutes before closing.

Pass/Permit/Fees: Walk-ins are free, and reservations are $109 per person.

Closest City or Town: New York City

Physical Address:
Patent Pending
49 W. 27th Street
New York, NY 10001

GPS Coordinates: 40.74607° N, 73.99019° W

Did You Know? Nikola Tesla lived and conducted his experiments in the building that houses the cocktail bar.

Pier 54: The *Titanic* Arrival Destination

Pier 59 was the original intended final destination of the *Titanic*. However, the survivors were picked up by the *Carpathia*, which took them to Pier 54. Thousands of people crowded the pier waiting for news of their loved ones.

Three years later in 1915, the *Lusitania* set sail from Pier 54. It was later torpedoed by a German U-boat off the coast of Ireland on May 7, sinking in just 20 minutes and killing almost all 2,000 passengers and crew. Pier 54 is now part of the Hudson River Park. It is currently a blank, empty strip of concrete and metal stretching out into the Hudson River.

Best Time to Visit: Pier 54 is available all year round for visitors.

Pass/Permit/Fees: There is no fee associated with this location.

Closest City or Town: New York City

Physical Address:
Cunard White Star Pier/Pier 54
55 E. River Piers
New York, NY 10004

GPS Coordinates: 40.74461° N, 74.00918° W

Did You Know? On May 6, 1932, a five-alarm fire destroyed Pier 54 and it had to be completely rebuilt.

Preserved Remnants of 17th-Century New York

The Portal Down to Old New York is near Broad and Pearl streets. At the pedestrian plaza of 85 Broad Street, there is a glass walkway that covers the remains of Colonial-Era New York. These remnants are some of the only relics of the old Dutch colony in Manhattan. They date back to when the city stretched just a little farther north from this location. The preserved site is located across from the Fraunces Tavern. It displays some of the oldest buildings in New York City, including part of colonial City Hall. The remnants of Lovelace Tavern are nearby, which date back to 1670.

Best Time to Visit: The best time to visit is during spring, summer, or fall when there is no snow on the ground and visitors will be able to look through the glass walkway without obstructions.

Pass/Permit/Fees: Tours are optional and cost between $29 and $35. It's free to view them independently.

Closest City or Town: New York City

Physical Address:
Portal Down to Old New York
63 Pearl Street
New York, NY 10004

GPS Coordinates: 40.70456° N, 74.01080° W

Did You Know? The remnants were discovered in 1975 during an excavation in Manhattan.

72

Secret Garden at St. Luke in the Fields

The Secret Garden at St. Luke in the Fields surrounds a picturesque church. While it is privately owned, the garden is made available to the public. Because cell phone use is not allowed, it is a quiet and reflective place. Most visitors go to read, journal, or just sit and reflect. It's home to 100 different species of birds and 24 different types of butterflies. The garden is centered on a yellowwood tree with paths branching off, and it rests on a 2-acre city block. Visitors can view the remains of the former parish that burned in a fire in 1981 as well as the Church of St. Luke. While walking through the gate, visitors will find the overwhelming noise of West Village simply falls away to nothing.

Best Time to Visit: The best time to visit is in the spring when the birds and butterflies are most active.

Pass/Permit/Fees: There are no fees associated with this location.

Closest City or Town: New York City

Physical Address:
Secret Garden at St. Luke in the Fields
487 Hudson Street
New York, NY 10014

GPS Coordinates: 40.73940° N, 74.00735° W

Did You Know? In 1842, a planting from England's Glastonbury tree was placed in the garden where it stood until 1990 when it was knocked down by storms.

Septuagesimo Uno

Septuagesimo Uno is often referred to as the smallest park in New York City despite the existence of smaller parks. It was built in the late 1960s as part of the Vest Pocket Park campaign that sought to bring green spaces to the lots between buildings. It only occupies 0.04 acres between two townhouses. Located on 71st Street, its name means "seventy-first" in Latin. The park is hard to find, and once one arrives, there is not much to do other than sit and relax. Because of this, it receives little traffic and is sought after for quiet, meditative reflection. It was officially opened in 1981 by the NYC Department of Parks & Recreation. In 2000, a $14,000 restoration project contributed the gates as well as other things to make the park what it is today. In that same year, it received its current name, replacing the original name of The 71st Street Plot.

Best Time to Visit: It's best to visit in the warmer months when it is comfortable enough to sit and enjoy the space.

Pass/Permit/Fees: There is no fee associated with this location.

Closest City or Town: New York City

Physical Address:
Septuagesimo Uno
W. 71st Street and West End Avenue
New York, NY 10023

GPS Coordinates: 40.77944° N, 73.98433° W

Did You Know? The park was acquired by the city on March 28, 1969, when the location was condemned.

Smallpox Memorial Hospital

In the 1800s, smallpox patients were kept isolated from the general population while they were being treated. On the tip of Blackwell's Island, which is now known as Roosevelt Island, New York City's smallpox hospital was built. Construction was completed in 1856 by labor obtained from the nearby mental asylum. Between 1856 and 1875, the hospital treated roughly 7,000 patients each year. In 1875, the hospital was converted to a nurses' dormitory because the island had become more populated. By the 1950s, it became abandoned and fell into disrepair. In 1975, the hospital was declared a city landmark, and the walls were reinforced to prevent it from completely falling down. The hospital was never renovated or opened for indoor tours. Today, all that remains are some of the outer walls and the foundation.

Best Time to Visit: It's best to visit Smallpox Memorial Hospital during the spring, summer, and fall on days when the weather is pleasant.

Pass/Permit/Fees: There are no fees.

Closest City or Town: New York City

Physical Address:
Smallpox Memorial Hospital
E. Road
New York, NY 10044

GPS Coordinates: 40.75310° N, 73.95813° W

Did You Know? The hospital is New York City's only landmarked ruin.

Statue of Liberty

The Statue of Liberty was a gift to the United States from France. It is universally recognized as a symbol of freedom and democracy. The statue was designed with a lot of symbolism. Her crown represents light, with the spikes indicating light shooting out. The tablet she's holding is inscribed with July 4, 1776, to represent Independence Day, and a broken shackle and chains at her feet represent the end of slavery in the country. The crown bears seven spikes, one for each sea and continent. In 1924, it was designated as a National Monument. There are 215 steps from the bottom to the top of the pedestal. There's also an elevator for those who are unable to use the stairs, but it is limited to one person per trip. Crown access is currently restricted.

Best Time to Visit: Visitor traffic to the monument is moderate during the fall, and visitors will find the queue lines shorter. Alternatively, the weather is nicer in June.

Pass/Permit/Fees: Admission is $23.50 for adults and $12 for children.

Closest City or Town: New York City

Physical Address:
Statue of Liberty
Liberty Island
New York, NY 10004

GPS Coordinates: 40.68926° N, 74.04450° W

Did You Know? The statue represents Libertas, the Roman goddess of freedom.

Statue of Liberty Museum

The Statue of Liberty Museum opened in 2019. It was built to replace the small gallery that stood in the pedestal of the statue itself. The museum contains 26,000 square feet of interactive exhibits, including a multitude of American heirlooms. The museum allows visitors to explore the magnificence of the statue without the need for advance reservations or tickets. The Immersive Theater is a 10-minute multimedia experience that allows visitors to experience the story of the Statue of Liberty's history and watch a virtual fly-through of the statue. The Engagement Gallery provides an inside look into the fabrication, design, and construction of the statue. The Inspiration Gallery is a place to reflect on the experiences of the museum. Additionally, the original torch is located in this gallery. The rooftop deck offers views of the statue and New York Harbor.

Best Time to Visit: The Statue of Liberty Museum is open daily from 8:30 a.m. to 5 p.m.

Pass/Permit/Fees: There are no fees to enter the museum.

Closest City or Town: New York City

Physical Address:
Statue of Liberty Museum
Liberty Island
New York, NY 10004

GPS Coordinates: 40.69760° N, 74.04611° W

Did You Know? Frédéric Auguste Bartholdi and a team of artisans built the statue.

St. Paul's Chapel

St. Paul's Chapel is located directly across the street from the World Trade Center site. When the attack on the Twin Towers occurred, the chapel miraculously incurred no structural damage at all. The chapel became a place for rescue workers to rest and recover during the many days they searched for survivors.

St. Paul's was first opened in 1766 as an outreach chapel of the Trinity Church. In the Great Fire of 1776, the Trinity Church burned to the ground along with a large portion of lower Manhattan. Many people, including George Washington, made St. Paul's Chapel their home church until 1790 when the second Trinity Church was built. The chapel was named a National Historic Landmark in 1960 and a New York City landmark in 1966.

Best Time to Visit: The chapel is open daily from 8:30 a.m. to 6 p.m.

Pass/Permit/Fees: There is no fee associated with this location.

Closest City or Town: New York City

Physical Address:
St. Paul's Chapel
209 Broadway
New York, NY 10007

GPS Coordinates: 40.71224° N, 74.00918° W

Did You Know? The chapel is the only remaining colonial structure in Manhattan.

Tannen's Magic Shop

Tannen's Magic Shop is the oldest magic shop in the country. It was first opened in 1925 in Manhattan. When the shop first started, it consisted of stands all over the city. Its first physical location was the Wurlitzer Building, but it's now located in a plain office building on 34th Street. For the last 90 years, it has supplied almost every famous magician. The magic tricks in the shop are divided into categories to make things easier for visitors, including groups like coin magic, card magic, and stage magic, among others. The employees will demonstrate some of the magic tricks for skeptical and curious visitors. The shop offers magic classes for those who are especially eager to learn the tricks of the trade. Tannen's also offers a weeklong summer camp for magic lovers. The camp was started in 1974 and accommodates over 130 students.

Best Time to Visit: The magic shop is open Monday through Friday from 11 a.m. to 6 p.m. and Saturday from 10 a.m. to 4 p.m.

Pass/Permit/Fees: There are no fees to visit this location.

Closest City or Town: New York City

Physical Address:
Tannen's Magic
45 W. 34th Street #608
New York, NY 10001

GPS Coordinates: 40.75048° N, 73.98692° W

Did You Know? The shop is located near the former residence of magician Harry Houdini.

The Battery

Castle Garden became the first immigrant depot of the world in 1855. The garden was originally built as the Southwest Battery in anticipation of the War of 1812; however, it never had the opportunity to fire upon the enemy. When beekeeping in New York City became legal in 2011, The Battery's BeeVillage was erected. It consists of small bee habitats designed to look like historic buildings. The Urban Farm at The Battery is the only public urban farm in Manhattan. It is used for educational purposes and features an outdoor classroom for students at participating schools as well as workshops and volunteer programs for the general public. *The Sphere* sculpture is now located in The Battery. It was recovered from the rubble following the attack on the World Trade Center.

Best Time to Visit: The best time to visit The Battery is between May and October.

Pass/Permit/Fees: There are no fees associated with this location.

Closest City or Town: New York City

Physical Address:
Statue of Liberty View Point
Battery Park Underpass
New York, NY 10004

GPS Coordinates: 40.70111° N, 74.01516° W

Did You Know? Pier A in The Battery is the home of the first permanent WWI memorial, which consists of a ship clock and bell that were installed in the watchtower.

The Elevated Acre

The Elevated Acre is a secret garden hidden at 55 Water Street on top of a parking garage. It is a 1-acre meadow surrounded by gardens. Featuring an amphitheater, a summer beer garden, and paths made of Brazilian hardwood, the Elevated Acre will offer visitors solitude. At the height the garden rests, the noise from below is almost completely gone, leaving visitors to relax in peace. They will also be able to experience amazing views of the Brooklyn Bridge and the East River. The entrance is a hard-to-find escalator, but it is well worth the hunt. The park offers itself as a venue for weddings, lunch breaks, and an ice rink in the winter. It is one of a handful of elevated privately owned public spaces. In the summer, outdoor movies are often hosted in the amphitheater area.

Best Time to Visit: The best time to visit the Elevated Acre is in the summer months when the weather is warmer.

Pass/Permit/Fees: There are no fees to visit this location.

Closest City or Town: New York City

Physical Address:
Elevated Acre
55 Water Street
New York, NY 10041

GPS Coordinates: 40.70423° N, 74.00885° W

Did You Know? The garden was built in 2005 when buildings in the city were given approval to add levels if they included a public plaza.

The Evolution Store

Located in the SoHo district, the Evolution Store is a place to find one-of-a-kind natural-history collectibles. Opened in 1993 when the owner decided to share his collection with the public, the shop is full of merchandise like framed butterflies and insects, fossils, seashells, and medical models and posters. The staff members are engaging and knowledgeable, and they're eager to answer questions about the store's merchandise. The merchandise is supplied by the same kinds of collectibles dealers that service museums. Visitors will have the option to browse and buy carnivorous plants, bugs under glass, taxidermized animal heads, chunks of coral, ammonite fossils, and stuffed rattlesnakes. There is almost no end to the oddities that can be seen and acquired for personal collections.

Best Time to Visit: The store is open Sunday through Saturday from 11 a.m. to 7 p.m.

Pass/Permit/Fees: There is no fee to browse, but purchasing merchandise will cost money.

Closest City or Town: New York City

Physical Address:
The Evolution Store
687 Broadway
New York, NY 10012

GPS Coordinates: 40.72898° N, 73.99484° W

Did You Know? The store sells candy made with real bugs as ingredients.

The Museum of Interesting Things

The Museum of Interesting Things is a mobile museum that travels to different locations, mostly schools, to offer interactive exhibits to viewers. It displays more than 300 curios and antiques dating back to the1800s, all curated by one man named Denny Daniel. The collection contains objects like rare books, mechanical toys, quack medical instruments, and many others. The exhibits are categorized by math, science, etc. Although it is a traveling museum, visitors have the option to book a private tour at its home location. Unlike most museums, viewers are encouraged to handle the antiques. The idea behind the museum is to educate visitors that things like their cell phones did not just appear but, instead, evolved over time.

Best Time to Visit: Viewings are typically between 10 a.m. and 6 p.m. but will vary based on show location. All viewings must be set up in advance.

Pass/Permit/Fees: Admission is $15.

Closest City or Town: New York City

Physical Address:
The Museum of Interesting Things
Georgetown Plaza
60 E. 8th Street
New York, NY 10003

GPS Coordinates: 40.73117° N, 73.99271° W

Did You Know? The museum's main location is in a private apartment.

The New York Earth Room

The New York Earth Room has a 22-inch layer of dirt spread on the floor across all 3,600 square feet, reaching a total of 280,000 pounds of soil. American artist Walter de Maria created the room in 1977. It was one of three, with the other two in Germany, but it is now the only one remaining. The piece explores links between art and the natural environment. The room is soothing and quiet, providing an escape from the everyday bustle of the city streets. To maintain the piece, curators have to regularly water the soil. Occasionally, mushrooms sprout up. The estimated value of the room is $1 million. The dirt covers three gallery rooms, and a plexiglass barrier on the side allows visitors to see how deep the dirt really is.

Best Time to Visit: Visit the Earth Room Wednesday through Sunday from 12 p.m. to 3 p.m. or 3:30 p.m. to 6 p.m.

Pass/Permit/Fees: There is no fee associated with this location.

Closest City or Town: New York City

Physical Address:
The Earth Room
141 Wooster Street
New York, NY 10012

GPS Coordinates: 40.72692° N, 73.99999° W

Did You Know? Bill Dilworth, the exhibit's caretaker for the last 30 years, waters and rakes the dirt once a week.

The Ramble Cave

The Ramble gives the appearance of being the most natural-looking location in New York. Central Park's planners, Frederick Law Olmsted and Calvert Vaux, put in hours of construction to create a rustic landscape. While the park is constantly changing, there are some locations within that remain the same. One such location is the Ramble Cave. The cave was not part of the original plan for the development of Central Park. When constructing the Ramble, they had to perform a lot of excavation. During a dig, they discovered a vein of rich mold. As it was carried away, a narrow cavity was revealed that did not meet the look the developers were going for. They added rocks and a staircase to give it the appearance that it has today. Visitors who don't know the steps are there may walk right by them because they are so well-obscured.

Best Time to Visit: The best time to visit the Ramble Cave is in the spring when the flowers are in bloom.

Pass/Permit/Fees: There is no fee associated with this location.

Closest City or Town: New York City

Physical Address:
The Ramble Cave
79th Street Transverse
New York, NY 10024

GPS Coordinates: 40.77871° N, 73.97138° W

Did You Know? Both entrances to the cave were sealed in the 1930s.

The SeaGlass Carousel

The SeaGlass Carousel is located in The Battery and housed in a glass-paneled nautilus shell on top of the location of the original New York Aquarium. Although the carousel opened in 2015, it took 10 years and several million dollars for The Battery Conservancy and George Tsypin to bring it to life. Featuring 30 fiberglass fish and 12 different species, the carousel does not have individual poles for each rider. Each fish is modeled after a real species and stands up to 95 feet wide by 13 feet tall. With the motors underneath the floor, visitors are offered the immersive experience of spinning and swirling around one other. Additionally, views are unobstructed because there are no central poles. Riders get the experience of becoming the fish as they ride inside them, not on top of them.

Best Time to Visit: The ride is open Sunday through Saturday from 11 a.m. to 9 p.m.

Pass/Permit/Fees: Admission is $5.50 per person or $50 for 10 tickets.

Closest City or Town: New York City

Physical Address:
SeaGlass Carousel
Water and State Street
New York, NY 10004

GPS Coordinates: 40.70224° N, 74.01491° W

Did You Know? Each fish is individually illuminated with color-changing LED lights and outfitted with audio systems.

The Sisyphus Stones

Uliks Gryka designed the Sisyphus Stones in July 2017. The rocks are not glued or cemented in place, so visitors are cautioned to keep small children away. These stone people are located on the Hudson River Greenway in Fort Washington Park. Gryka was inspired when he noticed that some of the stones appeared to have faces. As he began building them, for him, it was like telling their story.

Initially, the stones had a fluid and unpredictable appearance, disappearing completely some days, typically being toppled by vandals. Today, the stones have a more permanent place in the landscape. Locals and passersby have largely taken to rebuilding the stones. The site is marked by handmade signs.

Best Time to Visit: The Sisyphus Stones site is available all year round but is best enjoyed in the warmer months when the air coming off the water isn't so cold.

Pass/Permit/Fees: There is no fee associated with this location.

Closest City or Town: New York City

Physical Address:
Sisyphus Stones
Fort Washington Park
New York, NY 10032

GPS Coordinates: 40.84611° N, 73.94608° W

Did You Know? The glittering rock the stones are made of is Manhattan schist, a type of metamorphic rock.

The Treasures in the Trash Collection

The Treasures in the Trash Collection was curated over the course of Nelson Molina's 34 years with the NYC Department of Sanitation. It's located in Manhattan 11, an active sanitation garage that services East Harlem and contains over 40,000 items. The collection is a reminder that there are alternatives to waste, as Molina worked tirelessly to rescue, repair, and organize all of these discarded objects. Visitors will be treated to a visual reminder of the scale of what people throw away. The collection also offers stories of Harlem, Nelson's life, and New York City. The collection has no formal organization, but Molina tends to group items by size, general theme, and color.

Best Time to Visit: Tours must be scheduled with the city in advance.

Pass/Permit/Fees: There is no fee associated with this location.

Closest City or Town: New York City

Physical Address:
Treasures in the Trash
343 E. 99th Street
New York, NY 10029

GPS Coordinates: 40.78632° N, 73.94393° W

Did You Know? Sanitation workers are not allowed to take anything from the trash home for personal use, but they are allowed to keep it at work.

Times Square

Times Square was originally known as Long Acre Square and served as the site of William H. Vanderbilt's American Horse Exchange. In the late 1880s, it was just an open space surrounded by plain tenements. In 1904, it was renamed Times Square when it became the home of *The New York Times*. Today, it is surrounded by glowing billboards, high-rise buildings, and iconic locations. Home to the famous New Year's Eve celebrations that are watched around the world since 1907, Times Square is a household name. It is also home to the Broadway Theater, and the square is actually two triangles that are bisected by Broadway. The bright lights of the area can even be seen from outer space. Visitors will find sites like the Hard Rock Café, MTV, Planet Hollywood, and more at Times Square.

Best Time to Visit: The best time to visit Times Square is in the morning when the crowds are smaller.

Pass/Permit/Fees: There are no fees to visit this location.

Closest City or Town: New York City

Physical Address:
Official NYC Information Center, Times Square
W. 44th and W. 45th Street
New York, NY 10036

GPS Coordinates: 40.75710° N, 73.98576° W

Did You Know? There is a regulation for buildings in the Times Square area that requires them to have a certain amount of display lighting in order to preserve the area's reputation for glamour.

Titanic Memorial Park

The Titanic Memorial Lighthouse is located at the Titanic Memorial Park. The Unsinkable Molly Brown insisted that it be erected in honor of those who died during the nautical tragedy. It was originally built on top of the Seaman's Church Institute in 1913 but now resides at the entrance to the South Street Seaport. The lighthouse is 60 feet tall and was built the year after the sinking of the *Titanic*. A time ball was installed above the lighthouse, and it dropped daily at noon as a remembrance of those who were lost. In 1967, the ball stopped keeping time. It was at this point that the lighthouse was moved to its current location. The structure has a small park situated around it where visitors can rest. There is a project planned to restore the lighthouse to its original 1913 condition with a working time ball and green light. There is a petition for it to be named a National Historic Landmark.

Best Time to Visit: The best time to visit Titanic Memorial Park is on a nice warm day.

Pass/Permit/Fees: There are no fees.

Closest City or Town: New York City

Physical Address:
Titanic Memorial Park
Pearl Street
New York, NY 10038

GPS Coordinates: 40.70830° N, 74.00373° W

Did You Know? The time ball was activated by a telegraphic signal from Washington, D.C.

United Palace Theatre

The United Palace Theatre was built in 1930 as one of Loew's Wonder Theaters. Offering more than 3,000 seats, it is the fourth-largest venue of its kind in Manhattan. In 1969, the theatre's first 40 years of storytelling came to an end. Many theatres in the city were slated for demolition, but a church group known as the United Palace of Spiritual Arts purchased the building to continue its legacy. The theatre itself occupies an entire city block.

Today, it functions as both a spiritual center and a nonprofit cultural and performing-arts center. Its original intended purpose was to show films, but vaudeville acts were also performed here. In 2016, the building was designated a New York City landmark.

Best Time to Visit: Showtimes vary, and tickets must be purchased for entry. Visitors will need to plan their trips in advance.

Pass/Permit/Fees: Fees are based on the show selected and will vary on a show-by-show basis.

Closest City or Town: New York City

Physical Address:
United Palace
4140 Broadway
New York, NY 10033

GPS Coordinates: 40.84738° N, 73.93797° W

Did You Know? The United Palace Theatre has a capacity of 3,327 people.

Niagara Falls State Park

Located around Niagara Falls, the state park offers visitors a variety of excellent attractions to choose from. There is a no-fly zone under 3,500 feet located over the park, so all drone activity is strictly prohibited and no permits will be issued. The Visitor's Center coordinates park information and sells tickets for attractions like the Scenic Trolley that takes visitors on a 30-minute tour. The Cave of the Winds allows visitors to journey under the falls to the Hurricane Deck. The Observation Tower is the only United States location that allows visitors to observe both the American and Horseshoe falls. The Niagara Aquarium houses over 1,500 different species from the Great Lakes to the coral reefs.

Best Time to Visit: The best time to visit Niagara Falls State Park is June through August.

Pass/Permit/Fees: It is free to enter and look at the falls. There are other attractions that cost a fee per person.

Closest City or Town: Niagara Falls

Physical Address:
Niagara Falls State Park
332 Prospect Street
Niagara Falls, NY 14303

GPS Coordinates: 43.09713° N, 79.03707° W

Did You Know? One-fifth of the world's fresh water is in the four upper Great Lakes. All the outflow of this water eventually cascades over the falls as it travels down the Niagara River.

Niagara Falls Underground Railroad Heritage Center

The Niagara Falls Underground Railroad Heritage Center is located in the 1863 U.S. Customs House. The Customs House is adjacent to the location of the former International Suspension Bridge, which is where many people traveling the Underground Railroad crossed. The center opened for visitors in May 2018. The museum features stories from travelers on the Underground Railroad as well as abolitionists from Niagara Falls. The Customs House, not the Heritage Center, is on the National Register of Historic Places.

Best Time to Visit: Visitors can stop by the center Thursday through Sunday from 10 a.m. to 5 p.m.

Pass/Permit/Fees: Admission is $10 for adults, $8 for seniors or students, $6 for children ages 6–12, and free for children under age 6.

Closest City or Town: Niagara Falls

Physical Address:
Niagara Falls Underground Railroad Heritage Center
825 Depot Avenue West
Niagara Falls, NY 14305

GPS Coordinates: 43.09846° N, 79.11946° W

Did You Know? The exhibition starts in the atrium of the Amtrak station to which the Underground Railroad Heritage Center is attached.

Fort Ontario State Historic Site

The current Fort Ontario is built on the ruins of the foundations of the three previous forts. From 1944 to 1946, the fort was the location of the only refugee camp in the United States for victims of the Holocaust. There is a cemetery on site with 77 graves of officers, soldiers, women, and children who lived at the fort. It is open from dawn until dusk year-round. In 1946, the fort was transferred to the state, and it housed WWII veterans and their families until 1953. It became a historic site in 1949. There are two sets of officers' quarters as well as barracks, a storehouse, guardhouses, and the powder magazine. The former parade grounds have been transformed into baseball diamonds and picnic facilities.

Best Time to Visit: The fort is open May through October and operates Wednesday through Saturday from 10 a.m. to 4:30 p.m. and Sunday from 12 p.m. to 4:30 p.m.

Pass/Permit/Fees: Admission is $4 for adults and free for children.

Closest City or Town: Oswego

Physical Address:
Fort Ontario State Historic Site
1 E. 4th Street
Oswego, NY 13126

GPS Coordinates: 43.46620° N, 76.50823° W

Did You Know? Fort Ontario hosts demonstrations and major events throughout the year, including battle re-enactments.

Safe Haven Holocaust Refugee Shelter

The Safe Haven Holocaust Refugee Shelter Museum retells the story of 982 refugees. These refugees were brought to the Fort Ontario Emergency Refugee Shelter in August 1944. Safe Haven was the only official program in the U.S. that focused on rescuing refugees from the Holocaust. The group was placed in Fort Ontario behind barbed wire. They were given no status and were told they had no rights when it came to entering the United States because they would be returned to their home countries following the war. However, due to the political post-war climate, the refugees were offered the option to stay in the country. When they chose the refugees who would stay at Safe Haven, they decided that the ones selected must have no other option for a haven and should primarily be women and children.

Best Time to Visit: Visit from Memorial Day to Labor Day from 11 a.m. to 4 p.m. on weekends only or 11 a.m. to 4 p.m. Thursday through Sunday for the rest of the year.

Pass/Permit/Fees: Admission is $5 for adults and $3 for children or students.

Closest City or Town: Oswego

Physical Address:
Safe Haven
2 E. 7th Street
Oswego, NY 13126

GPS Coordinates: 43.46446° N, 76.50437° W

Did You Know? Most of the refugees selected were from Yugoslavia.

Huckleberry Mountain

The Huckleberry Mountain Trail is 4.98 miles round trip, and the mountain itself is located in the Kaaterskill Mountain range. This hike is nice and not overly difficult, so hikers of all skill levels will enjoy this trail. Visitors should follow the yellow trail signs all the way to the peak. The Catskills and the Hudson River are both visible at Huckleberry Point. There are streams, different sections of pine trees, and some steep ascents on the trail.

For visitors who go on rainy days, the streams may be difficult to pass. There are bears in the area, so it is recommended that anyone climbing the mountain brush up on their bear safety. The trail is clearly marked from the very start. Hikers will have to be careful because there is one point at which an unmarked road branches off from the marked trail, and they should avoid making the mistake of stepping away onto the wrong path.

Best Time to Visit: Visitors should plan their hike for days with no rain in the spring, summer, and fall.

Pass/Permit/Fees: There are no fees.

Closest City or Town: Phoenicia

Physical Address:
Huckleberry Point Trailhead
2425 Platte Clove Road
Elka Park, NY 12427

GPS Coordinates: 42.13651° N, 74.08244° W

Did You Know? The peak elevation is 2,545 feet.

Peekamoose Blue Hole

A popular swimming hole in the Catskills, Peekamoose Blue Hole gets a lot of visitors. The water's color changes depending on the time of day and the season. It can range from blue to emerald green. It's 20 feet deep in some locations, and the water is also always very cold, so visitors will not want to swim for extended periods of time.

Additionally, those with medical conditions may want to skip the water altogether to avoid complications. There are many good hiking trails near this location for those interested. The scenic 50-foot Buttermilk Falls is nearby, located within a mile of the swimming hole.

Best Time to Visit: Weekdays during the early mornings are the best times to visit. By 11 a.m., the site is usually crowded, and parking is no longer an option.

Pass/Permit/Fees: A $10 permit is required to visit.

Closest City or Town: Phoenicia

Physical Address:
Peekamoose Blue Hole
Peekamoose Road
Sundown, NY 12740

GPS Coordinates: 41.92956° N, 74.42726° W

Did You Know? This swimming hole is formed as a section of the Rondout Creek that flows into Rondout Reservoir. This reservoir is where over half of the drinking water in New York City originates.

Wittenberg Mountain

Wittenberg Mountain offers one of the best, most scenic lookouts in the Catskill Mountains. It is located in the Slide Mountain Wilderness Area and is part of the Burroughs Range. There are several different starting points visitors can take to the summit. The Woodland Valley start tends to be challenging for most people. Alternative routes can include hiking two other peaks: Cornell and Slide. The summit of Wittenberg Mountain is a large, open rock shelf. There is a wide-open view of the Ashokan Reservoir below. The trail from the Woodland Valley ascends 3.7 miles and returns down the mountain following the same route. The peak stands at 3,780 feet.

Best Time to Visit: Spring, summer, and fall offer the best times for hiking. It's recommended to go during the week as the trails are in high demand during the weekend.

Pass/Permit/Fees: When parking in Woodland Valley State Park, there is a $6 parking fee between May and October.

Closest City or Town: Phoenicia

Physical Address:
Wittenberg Mountain
961 Woodland Valley Road
Phoenicia, NY 12464

GPS Coordinates: 42.01179° N, 74.34694° W

Did You Know? Climbing Wittenberg Mountain is required to gain membership into the Catskill Mountain 3500 Club.

Flushing Meadows-Corona Park

Flushing Meadows-Corona Park was the site of two World's Fairs, one in 1939 and the other in 1964. The park is the largest in Queens, and the fourth-largest of its kind in all of New York City, featuring 900 acres of land. It offers access to a variety of sports, including baseball, tennis, soccer, and volleyball. There are also multiple lakes and trails that allow visitors to hike, bike, and kayak. Meadow Lake hosts the Hong Kong Dragon Boat Festival, and the park itself hosts the Queens Night Market in the summer. The Queens Museum is also located inside the park. It was built in 1972 to be an art museum and educational center. Visitors will also have the option to visit the Queens Zoo, the Queens Theatre in the Park, and the Flushing River. One of the country's first science museums, the New York Hall of Science, still operates in its original location.

Best Time to Visit: The best time to visit Flushing Meadows-Corona Park is in spring, summer, or fall when the weather is nice.

Pass/Permit/Fees: Entry to the park itself is free. Activities inside will have costs associated with them.

Closest City or Town: Queens

Physical Address:
14 Ederle Promenade
Flushing, NY 11367

GPS Coordinates: 40.74018° N, 73.84032° W

Did You Know? The park was once home to a large ash dump and was consider nothing more than wasteland.

Wildlife Freedom Foundation

The Wildlife Freedom Foundation is a pet and rescue shelter in New York City. Their mission is to rescue and place strays as well as rehabilitate wildlife. They boast three cat sanctuaries, all located on Roosevelt Island. The largest is the most well-known and a site that tourists will want to visit. It houses 22 very happy, formerly stray cats. They were all once from neglected or abusive situations. Now, they are up to date on vaccinations, have been spayed or neutered, and are healthy. All the cats have names. The idea behind the sanctuary started in 2004 with a group who was devastated by the loss of a local cat named Princess Yin Yang. The group sought to develop a plan to trap, neuter, and release all the stray cats of the area and then find homes for all of them.

Best Time to Visit: Visitors are welcome Sunday, Monday, Tuesday, Thursday, and Saturday from 12 p.m. to 6 p.m.; on Wednesday from 11:30 a.m. to 6 p.m.; and Friday from 11:30 a.m. to 6:30 p.m.

Pass/Permit/Fees: WFF requests donations for support.

Closest City or Town: Queens

Physical Address:
1 Southpoint Park
Roosevelt Island
New York, NY 10044

GPS Coordinates: 40.76434° N, 73.96048° W

Did You Know? There is a feral cat colony down the road in an abandoned smallpox hospital.

Lake Ontario

Lake Ontario is the smallest and easternmost of the Great Lakes. It is bordered in the north by Ontario and in the south by New York. Canada was covered by the Laurentide Glacier, which began melting 14,000 years ago. In its wake, it created Lake Iroquois, which was the much-larger predecessor of Lake Ontario. As the glacier thawed in the St. Lawrence River valley, Lake Iroquois's water flowed out to the Atlantic, leaving behind Lake Admiralty. Eventually, this lake's bedrock settled, creating Lake Ontario. All the water from all the Great Lakes makes its way through Lake Ontario before it continues on to the Atlantic Ocean. The lake features a natural rhythm with its water moving back and forth every 11 minutes. Lake Ontario is the 14th-largest lake in the entire world.

Best Time to Visit: The best time to visit Lake Ontario is between May and October. These months offer the most beautiful weather in the area.

Pass/Permit/Fees: There are no fees associated with this location.

Closest City or Town: Rochester

Physical Address:
Ontario Beach Park
50 Beach Avenue
Rochester, NY 14612

GPS Coordinates: 43.60210° N, 77.62117° W

Did You Know? Because the lake is so deep, it never completely freezes.

Ganondagan State Historic Site

The Ganondagan State Historic Site is the only New York State Historic Site devoted to a Native American theme and the only Seneca town developed and maintained in the U.S. The site features a full-size longhouse that is furnished in the traditional way. There is also the Seneca Art & Culture Center. This center features information about the art and cultural influences of the Iroquois. There are two interpretive trails on the grounds surrounding the center. They focus on educating visitors about plant life and Haudenosaunee culture and history.

Best Time to Visit: The best time to visit Ganondagan State Historic Site is during the spring and summer from Wednesday through Saturday from 9 a.m. to 4 p.m.

Pass/Permit/Fees: From May 1 to October 31, admission is $8 for adults, $4 for students or seniors, $2 for children ages 5–11, and free for children under 5. During the remainder of the year, admission is $6 for adults, $3 for seniors or students, $1 for children ages 5–11, and free for children under 5.

Closest City or Town: Rochester

Physical Address:
Ganondagan State Historic Site
1488 NY-444
Victor, NY 14564

GPS Coordinates: 42.96401° N, 77.41410° W

Did You Know? Ganondagan is the site of a 17th-century Seneca town.

Susan B. Anthony Museum & House

This location was the home of Susan B. Anthony, the civil rights leader. It's also where she was arrested for voting in 1872. She was the president of the National American Woman Suffrage Association and ran the headquarters out of her home. Her home is also the site of her death in 1906. Anthony became an activist in 1849. Before and during the Civil War, she traveled throughout New York organizing abolitionist meetings. She joined with Elizabeth Cady Stanton in 1869 to form a militant wing of the women's rights movement. The museum collects artifacts and research materials related to her life and legacy and makes them readily available to the public through tours, publications, and the internet. It is a not-for-profit organization made possible through the generosity of donors and members.

Best Time to Visit: The museum and house are open Tuesday through Sunday from 11 a.m. to 5 p.m.

Pass/Permit/Fees: Admission is $15 for adults, $10 for seniors, and $5 for students.

Closest City or Town: Rochester

Physical Address:
Susan B. Anthony Museum & House
17 Madison Street
Rochester, NY 14608

GPS Coordinates: 43.15393° N, 77.62802° W

Did You Know? Susan B. Anthony was the first woman featured on U.S. currency.

Susan B. Anthony Square

The main focal point of the Susan B. Anthony Square Park is a sculpture known as *Let's Have Tea*. It features Anthony and Frederick Douglass, another pioneer of civil rights. These two historical figures are seated at a table, sharing a pot of tea. The sculpture was created by Pepsy Kettavong, a local Rochester sculptor, and erected in 2001. The park is located off West Main Street, just west of downtown. It offers visitors a place to rest after seeing the Susan B. Anthony Museum and House.

Best Time to Visit: It's better to visit Susan B. Anthony Square during the summer months when the weather is warm.

Pass/Permit/Fees: There are no fees associated with this location.

Closest City or Town: Rochester

Physical Address:
Susan B. Anthony Square
31 Madison Street
Rochester, NY 14608

GPS Coordinates: 43.15490° N, 77.62727° W

Did You Know? It was uncommon in their day for men and women to be friends, which makes this sculpture a testament to the barriers that Anthony and Douglass broke during their lifetimes.

Allegany State Park

With its two developed areas, Quaker and Red House, Allegany State Park is the largest state park in New York. Both offer visitors sandy beaches, museums, and trails. Red House is available to walkers and bikers with 5 miles of paved trails. There are 18 hiking trails in total throughout the entire park, with three developed as self-guided nature trails.

In the winter, visitors can go to the Art Roscoe Ski Touring Area for exceptional cross-country skiing trails that convert to excellent bike trails in the summer. Snowmobilers are also drawn to the 90 miles of snowmobile trails. There are several other activities offered, including bird watching, fishing, hunting, canoeing, and horseback riding. For those wanting an extended stay, there are 424 campsites, 375 cabins, and three group camps available for rent.

Best Time to Visit: It's best to visit Allegany State Park in the fall when the foliage is full of vibrant color.

Pass/Permit/Fees: Vehicle entry fees start at $6.

Closest City or Town: Salamanca

Physical Address:
Allegany State Park
2373 ASP, US-1
Salamanca, NY 14779

GPS Coordinates: 42.07919° N, 78.77108° W

Did You Know? Allegany State Park covers approximately 65,000 acres.

Lake George

Lake George offers 109 miles of shoreline and over 300 islands. Main attractions include the beaches, fishing, and riding on the water in a paddleboat, pontoon, or canoe. The area also has many forts, museums, and public parks. Lake George is full of history since it was the site of major battles during the French and Indian War. Visitors can view monuments at Battlefield Park or listen to ghost stories at Fort William Henry.

It is also the site of Six Flags Great Escape and Hurricane Harbor. This amusement park is one of the largest in the state. In 2019, Dino Roar Valley opened. It features a *Jurassic Park*-like motif with life-sized dinosaurs. It is open seasonally from the spring through the fall. Lake George also features the Adirondack Extreme Adventure Course, which is open April through November and offers 1.5 miles of treetop rope courses.

Best Time to Visit: The best time to visit Lake George is spring through fall.

Pass/Permit/Fees: Fees vary by activity.

Closest City or Town: Saratoga Springs

Physical Address:
Million Dollar Beach
139 Beach Road
Lake George, NY 12845

GPS Coordinates: 43.41727° N, 73.70414° W

Did You Know? Rachel Ray grew up in Lake George.

Moreau Lake State Park

Moreau Lake State Park is comprised of 4,100 acres. Its lake is located within a mix of hardwoods, pines, and rocky ridges. The Hudson River also flows through the park, offering visitors the option to kayak. The park features over 20 miles of hiking trails.

The park also hosts two pavilions with capacities of up to 120 people and a 20-foot by 30-foot tent with a capacity of up to 50 people. All three of these can be rented daily for events. Depending on the season, hiking, swimming, cross-country skiing, boating, fishing, and ice fishing are all available. Visitors can seasonally rent snowshoes, rowboats, paddleboards, and kayaks.

Best Time to Visit: Moreau Lake State Park is open all year.

Pass/Permit/Fees: Admission is $8 per car from May 28 to September 5. During the remainder of the year, admission is $6 per car on weekends and holidays only.

Closest City or Town: Saratoga Springs

Physical Address:
Moreau Lake State Park
605 Old Saratoga Road
Gansevoort, NY 12831

GPS Coordinates: 43.23601° N, 73.72010° W

Did You Know? Pico and Killington peaks in Vermont are visible from the park's Western Ridge Trail.

Saratoga Siege Trail

The Saratoga Siege Trail is an area of historical significance. In 1777, following their victory at the Battle of Saratoga, American soldiers pursued the British across Fish Creek. The British were surrounded and left with no option of escape. General John Burgoyne surrendered to the American army on October 17, 1777, swaying the French to join the Revolutionary War on the side of the Americans. Today, the location is a trail open to the public. Visitors are welcome to observe nature, snowshoe, walk, and cross-country ski. For safety reasons, the trail is closed during big-game hunting season. The trailhead is to the south of Schuyler House. It is half a mile long and connects Route 4 to Evans Street while following along the south side of Fish Creek. The trail is a scenic route through a mix of conifer and hardwood trees.

Best Time to Visit: The best time to visit this trail is June through August when the weather is warm but comfortable.

Pass/Permit/Fees: There are no fees associated with this location.

Closest City or Town: Saratoga Springs

Physical Address:
Saratoga Siege Trail
1060-1066 US-4
Schuylerville, NY 12871

GPS Coordinates: 42.99983° N, 73.63166° W

Did You Know? The trail crosses over both state and PLAN-owned land.

Saratoga Spa State Park

The Saratoga Spa State Park features many well-known institutions, including the Saratoga Performing Arts Center, the National Museum of Dance, and the Roosevelt Baths and Spa. It also has the Peerless Pool Complex, which has a main pool with zero-depth entry, a slide pool, and a children's pool. There is an alternative as well, called the Victoria Pool. The Saratoga Spa State Park Golf Course is made up of two courses: an 18-hole course and a challenging 9-hole course. Visitors are invited to run, walk, and bike throughout miles of nature trails. During the winter months, there are 12 miles of cross-country skiing and snowshoeing trails available. The park also features a classroom that runs year-round. It offers educational classes, hikes, tours, and more.

Best Time to Visit: There is something available during every season, making this a great park to visit at any time.

Pass/Permit/Fees: Admission is $10 for vehicles or special-event vehicles, $35 for nonprofit bus, and $75 for commercial buses.

Closest City or Town: Saratoga Springs

Physical Address:
Saratoga Spa State Park
19 Roosevelt Drive
Saratoga Springs, NY 12866

GPS Coordinates: 43.05497° N, 73.79940° W

Did You Know? Even though Geyser Creek runs through the park, there are no actual geysers located here.

Howe Caverns

Howe Caverns takes visitors on a journey 156 feet below the Earth's surface. Second to only Niagara Falls, it is one of the most popular natural attractions in New York. It features a 1.25-mile walk with a 0.25-mile boat ride, all underground. Visitors get to see amazing rock formations and ride on the underground river that created them.

Special tours are offered for additional fees. It is significantly colder underground, and visitors are recommended to wear warmer clothing for the duration of their tours. The standard tour lasts approximately 90 minutes.

Best Time to Visit: Tours are offered year round; however, visitors will want to arrive early to avoid crowds.

Pass/Permit/Fees: Admission is $25 for adults, $22 for seniors, $15 for children over the age of 4, and free for children under 4. Family Flashlight Tours are $45 per person, and a private tour with up to 36 people is $750. Specialty tours vary in price.

Closest City or Town: Schoharie

Physical Address:
Howe Caverns
255 Discovery Drive
Howes Cave, NY 12092

GPS Coordinates: 42.69712° N, 74.39860° W

Did You Know? Howe purchased the property for $100 in 1843.

Cayuga Lake State Park

Cayuga Lake State Park is located in the Finger Lakes region at the north end of the lake. The main highlight of this 188-acre park is its scenic view of Cayuga Lake.

The park offers a campground for tents and trailers for those visitors who want to stay over. There are also cabins for rent that have views of the lake. Visitors can relax on the beach or swim. Picnic tables, pavilions, and recreational programs are also available. There is a nature trail, a playground, and playing fields. In the winter, visitors can participate in snowshoeing, sledding, cross-country skiing, and ice fishing.

Best Time to Visit: The best time to visit Cayuga Lake State Park is May through September.

Pass/Permit/Fees: Admission is $7 for cars, $35 for noncommercial buses, $75 for commercial buses, and $75 for seasonal bus passes.

Closest City or Town: Seneca Falls

Physical Address:
Cayuga Lake State Park
2678 Lower Lake Road
Seneca Falls, NY 13148

GPS Coordinates: 42.92045° N, 76.75580° W

Did You Know? Lake Cayuga is 40 miles long, making it the longest of the Finger Lakes.

Elizabeth Cady Stanton Home

In 1848, Elizabeth Cady Stanton helped organize a Women's Rights Convention in Seneca Falls. This is largely regarded as the beginning of the modern feminist movement. One year prior, she and her husband moved with their children to Seneca Falls. She discovered that it was impossible for a woman to develop her full potential while burdened by the daily housework and childcare. It was this revelation that led her into the Women's Rights Movement. In addition to the site being significant as simply her home, this location also saw visits from such influential people as Frederick Douglass, Frances Dana Barker Gage, William Lloyd Garrison, and Matilda Joslyn Gage. The Stanton House is part of the Women's Rights National Historic Park.

Best Time to Visit: The park is open year round but closes on major holidays.

Pass/Permit/Fees: There are no fees associated with this location.

Closest City or Town: Seneca Falls

Physical Address:
Elizabeth Cady Stanton Home
32 Washington Street
Seneca Falls, NY 13148

GPS Coordinates: 42.91311° N, 76.78844° W

Did You Know? Elizabeth Cady Stanton raised five sons and two daughters in this home.

Montezuma National Wildlife Refuge

The Montezuma National Wildlife Refuge was established in 1938. Its goal was to return the area to its former state as marshland. The marshes had been previously drained, and all the wildlife followed the water. With the help of the Civilian Conservation Corp, a series of dikes were constructed and began to hold water, allowing the wildlife to return. Today, the refuge provides visitors with wildlife-dependent recreation, educational programs, and other public uses. The refuge is approximately 10,000 acres and located at the north end of Cayuga Lake. The refuge is home to many animals, including 60 eagles, muskrat, deer, mink, fox, coyote, and many kinds of birds. It is labeled as an Audubon Important Bird Area.

Best Time to Visit: Visiting in late February to April will overlap with the spring migration. Mid-April and May are the best times to visit to see hatching.

Pass/Permit/Fees: There is no fee associated with this location.

Closest City or Town: Seneca Falls

Physical Address:
Montezuma National Wildlife Refuge
3395 US-20
Seneca Falls, NY 13148

GPS Coordinates: 42.96360° N, 76.74103° W

Did You Know? More than 240 species of birds call the Montezuma NWR home throughout the course of the year.

Seneca Falls Historical Society

The Seneca Falls Historical Society was founded in 1896. It is located in a 23-room mansion that's supposedly haunted. The 10-acre property has a carriage house and a tool shed that's been remodeled into a General Store replica, along with a vineyard, garden, and orchard. This collection features archival records, unique documents, and artifacts. The historical society strives to bring about understanding of Seneca Falls's past as well its connection to the present. The museum, archives, and collections are readily available to the public. The mansion features Victorian-style rooms, local history exhibits, and an extensive research library. The society is also in possession of a series of glass plate negatives relating to the Women's Rights Movement.

Best Time to Visit: Visit from Monday through Friday from 9 a.m. to 4 p.m.

Pass/Permit/Fees: Admission is $10 for adults, $5 for children under 12, and $8 for veterans or AARP members. There is also a family package available with two adult tickets and two children's tickets for $25.

Closest City or Town: Seneca Falls

Physical Address:
Seneca Falls Historical Society
55 Cayuga Street
Seneca Falls, NY 13148

GPS Coordinates: 42.91607° N, 76.79496° W

Did You Know? The Seneca Falls Historical Society started out in a one-room schoolhouse.

Seneca Knitting Mill

The 1844 Seneca Knitting Mill building has been the location of the National Women's Hall of Fame since August 2020. The knitting mill is the sole surviving building of the town's time as the center of the Industrial Revolution. Originally constructed in 1844, it started as the Seneca Woolen Mill. Bought and sold many times over the years, the mill experienced several name changes. In 1860, it finally became the Seneca Knitting Mill and operated for 155 years until closing in 1999. Today, it features exhibits honoring the women who have been inducted into the Hall of Fame and tells their stories. The mill also hosts Induction Weekend, during which distinguished American women are celebrated for their contributions to society.

Best Time to Visit: Visit Seneca Knitting Mill any day except Wednesday between 11 a.m. and 4 p.m.

Pass/Permit/Fees: Admission is $7 for adults, $6 for seniors or military, $4 for children ages 12–18, and free for children under age 12. Members may also visit for free.

Closest City or Town: Seneca Falls

Physical Address:
Seneca Knitting Mill
1 Canal Street
Seneca Falls, NY 13148

GPS Coordinates: 42.90997 ° N, 76.79938 ° W

Did You Know? Two of the mill's trustees, Jacob Chamberlain and Charles Hoskins, signed the Declaration of Sentiments.

Women's Rights National Historical Park

The Women's Rights National Historical Park marks the site of the first Women's Rights Convention. The Wesleyan Chapel, the Women's Rights Museum, and the home of Elizabeth Cady Stanton are featured in the park. Three hundred women and 40 men attended the Convention in 1848. It is best known for the adoption of the Declaration of Sentiments. Frederick Douglass, notable abolitionist and former slave, attended and addressed the convention.

The Wesleyan Chapel was chosen as the site of the Women's Rights Convention due to its split from the Methodist Episcopal Church. The Wesleyans chose to take a more radical stance on opposing slavery than other Methodists. The chapel was routinely made available for reform speakers and events.

Best Time to Visit: This park is open all day year round.

Pass/Permit/Fees: There is no fee associated with this location.

Closest City or Town: Seneca Falls

Physical Address:
Women's Rights National Historical Park
136 Fall Street
Seneca Falls, NY 13148

GPS Coordinates: 42.91153° N, 76.80022° W

Did You Know? Seneca Falls's Wesleyan congregation was the first to build a chapel.

Panama Rocks Scenic Park

Panama Rocks Scenic Park features a ridge full of crevices and caves. Everything is enclosed in an ancient forest. There is a 1-mile hiking trail around the park, but many visitors will find they enjoy leaving the trail to explore. This trail is rated as a Class 1 hiking trail. However, visitors will still have to watch out for typical trail hazards like tree roots, and strollers or wheelchairs are not recommended. At Axcellent Adventures at Panama Rocks, visitors can throw axes. They offer competitions as well as additional games and activities. Glamping is available, and Camp at the Rocks accommodations include fully furnished 19-foot bell tents. Pets are not allowed for safety reasons.

Best Time to Visit: Visit from May through October.

Pass/Permit/Fees: Admission is $10 for adults, $7 for children, and free for children ages 5 and under. Season passes cost $16 for adults and $12 for children. Guests who order online receive a $1 discount on day passes and $2 discount on season passes for adults only.

Closest City or Town: Sherman

Physical Address:
Panama Rocks Scenic Park
11 Rock Hill Road
Panama, NY 14767

GPS Coordinates: 42.07387° N, 79.48784° W

Did You Know? The rock formations date back 350–400 million years ago.

Chittenango Falls

Chittenango Falls is home to many endangered and rare species of plants and animals. The Chittenango ovate amber snail only lives under the rocks found in and around the falls. The Hart's-tongue fern and roseroot can both be found growing on the gorge walls. These plants only grow in damp, rocky environments like this.

The falls come down in a cascade, almost like a staircase. They descend in even drops, one after the next. In the mid-1800s, the falls were the driving force of industry in Chittenango. Numerous factories and mills were built in the vicinity. The Chittenango Falls Park Association managed the park from 1887 to 1922, when it was turned over to the state. Since then, the state has increased the acreage to 194.

Best Time to Visit: Chittenango Falls is open year round.

Pass/Permit/Fees: Admission is $3 per car on weekdays and $5 per car on weekends or holidays. Fees may be waived in the off-season, and pedestrians are always welcome to enter for free.

Closest City or Town: Syracuse

Physical Address:
Chittenango Falls State Park
2300 Rathbun Road
Cazenovia, NY 13035

GPS Coordinates: 42.97843° N, 75.83668° W

Did You Know? The falls were created by glaciers that revealed 40-million-year-old layers of limestone.

Green Lakes State Park

The highlight of Green Lakes State Park is its two lakes that have waters like the Caribbean Sea. Round Lake and Green Lake are both meromictic, meaning their layers of water will never mix. With this type of lake, it is likely to find evidence of ancient flora and fauna. Due to the sensitive nature of the lakes, outside vessels are not allowed. The park features the 18-hole Green Lakes State Park Golf Course. Other activities include hiking, biking, fishing, and swimming. In the winter, visitors can snowshoe or cross-country ski. Green Lakes State Park officially became a state park in 1928 when it acquired its northern 500 acres. Further acquisitions expanded it to roughly 2,100 acres. In 1975, Round Lake was named a National Natural Landmark.

Best Time to Visit: The best time to visit Green Lakes State Park is during the spring, summer, or fall.

Pass/Permit/Fees: Admission is $10 for cars, $35 for noncommercial buses, $75 for commercial buses, or $75 for a seasonal bus pass.

Closest City or Town: Syracuse

Physical Address:
Green Lakes State Park
7900 Green Lakes Road
Fayetteville, NY 13066

GPS Coordinates: 43.06443° N, 75.97233° W

Did You Know? The park's glacial lakes were formed about 15,000 years ago at the end of the last ice age.

Harriet Tubman National Historic Park

The Harriet Tubman National Historic Park was established on January 10, 2017. It is located at the site where Harriet Tubman lived, worshiped, and cared for family members and formerly enslaved people. Tubman was known for her heroic efforts of bringing more than 300 people out of slavery.

As a commemoration of her life's work, the park includes the Harriet Tubman Residence, the Harriet Tubman Visitor Center, and the Tubman Home for the Aged. Additionally, the Thompson Memorial African Methodist Episcopal Zion Church, a 2-story structure built in 1891 where Tubman would worship, is also included in the 32-acre park.

Best Time to Visit: The Harriet Tubman National Historic Park is open year round from Tuesday through Sunday.

Pass/Permit/Fees: Admission is $5 for adults and $2 for children.

Closest City or Town: Syracuse

Physical Address:
Harriet Tubman National Historical Park
180 South Street
Auburn, NY 13021

GPS Coordinates: 42.91752° N, 76.56449° W

Did You Know? The land on which Tubman's home sits was sold to her in 1859 by then-Senator William H. Seward.

120

Salmon River Falls

The Salmon River Falls area encompasses 112 acres and is home to a 110-foot waterfall of the same name. Because of the area's popularity, the Department of Environmental Conservation has made a lot of improvements to the site. The main road, Falls Trail, is made of hard gravel and now accommodates the Americans with Disabilities Act. Disabled guests as well as parents with strollers can take advantage of the trail.

There are two overlooks along the main trail for visitors to view the falls. The first one provides a distant view while the second is closer. Additionally, there is the 600-foot Gorge Trail that descends 100 feet into the gorge of the falls. It offers the best view of the falls around halfway down.

Best Time to Visit: Salmon River Falls is open year round.

Pass/Permit/Fees: There is no fee to visit Salmon River Falls.

Closest City or Town: Syracuse

Physical Address:
Salmon River Falls Parking Area
185 Falls Road
Richland, NY 13144

GPS Coordinates: 43.54910° N, 75.94366° W

Did You Know? Water flow is controlled by a hydroelectric dam roughly 1 mile upstream from the falls.

Thousand Island Park Historic District

The Thousand Island Park Historic District contains numerous preserved structures from the late 19th and early 20th centuries. It includes 294 contributing buildings. The park is on the tip of Wellesley Island. It was founded in 1875 by Reverend J. F. Dayan as a place for families to obtain lots for tents or cottages for the summer season. In 1890, the park was well-established with 600 cottages.

The Centennial Celebration was held in 1975 to renew appreciation for the architecture and the setting. The celebration led to the creation of the Landmark Society the following year. This small group of society members succeeded in getting the Thousand Island Park Historic District listed on the National Register of Historic Places in 1982.

Best Time to Visit: Fall is a great time to visit this historic district because the crowds are much smaller.

Pass/Permit/Fees: Day parking is $7.25 for cars, $20.50 for vehicles with boat trailers, and $20.50 for buses.

Closest City or Town: Thousand Islands

Physical Address:
Thousand Island Park Historic District
Thousand Island Park, NY 13692

GPS Coordinates: 44.28871° N, 76.02773° W

Did You Know? A fire in 1912 destroyed the park's last great hotel, the Columbian, as well as 99 cottages and the business district.

Bear Mountain State Park

Bear Mountain State Park is located in the mountains rising off the west bank of the Hudson River. The park has many attractions, including lake and river fishing access, a large play field, and trails. Visitors can enjoy hiking, biking, and cross-country skiing, depending on the season. In the winter months, there is an outdoor rink for ice skating. The park also features the Trailside Museums and Zoo. This attraction has an Amphibian, Reptile, and Fish Museum with live specimens for visitors to observe. The Geology Museum gives visitors the prehistory of the Hudson Highlands. The Bear Mountain State Park Merry-Go-Round features 42 hand-carved seats made in the image of local animals.

Best Time to Visit: The best time to visit Bear Mountain State Park is during the warmer months of June through August.

Pass/Permit/Fees: Parking is $7. Pool admission is $2 for adults and $1 for children. Admission to the Trailside Museums and Zoo is $1 for adults and $0.50 for children.

Closest City or Town: Tomkins Cove

Physical Address:
Bear Mountain State Park
Route 9W North
Bear Mountain, NY 10911

GPS Coordinates: 41.38365° N, 73.99961° W

Did You Know? Bear Mountain got its name because its profile looks like a bear lying down.

Doodletown

Doodletown was a mining town near Bear Mountain. When the government decided to develop the mountain into a park, it used eminent domain to force out any remaining residents and demolished their houses. All that's left of the town are the foundations and walkways. Doodletown is best experienced as part of a hike, although visitors will have to be careful since the area is full of snakes of all kinds in the trees and on the ground. The old iron mine is accessible, but it is highly advisable that one does not enter it. It could be unstable or have a wild animal inside, making the location very dangerous.

Best Time to Visit: Doodletown is open year round.

Pass/Permit/Fees: There is no fee to visit this location.

Closest City or Town: Tomkins Cove

Physical Address:
Trailhead for Cornell Mine Trail and Doodletown Brook
Route 9W
Tomkins Cove, NY 10986

GPS Coordinates: 41.30417° N, 74.02770° W

Did You Know? In the 1890s, Thomas Edison bought an iron mine in Doodletown to run an experiment that later failed.

Chimney Bluffs State Park

Chimney Bluffs State Park is located just 2 miles from Lake Bluff Campground, making it the perfect spot to visit for campers. The park was formed by the advance of glaciers over 10,000 years ago. In the process of advancing, the glacier formed egg-shaped hills, or drumlins. This area has one of the largest drumlin fields in North America. Geologists estimate that the bluff retreats 5 feet every year from natural erosion and weathering. There are several trails available for visitors to hike. Swimming is prohibited, but fishing is allowed with a proper license. Kayaking and paddleboarding are also permitted. The park is open all year from dawn until dusk. In the winter months, the trails become cross-country ski and snowmobile trails.

Best Time to Visit: It's best to visit Chimney Bluffs State Park during the spring, summer, and fall months.

Pass/Permit/Fees: Admission is $5 per vehicle from April 1 to October 31.

Closest City or Town: Wolcott

Physical Address:
Chimney Bluffs State Park
7700 Garner Road
Wolcott, NY 14590

GPS Coordinates: 43.28235° N, 76.92233° W

Did You Know? During Prohibition, Canadian smugglers would drop off liquor in the Chimney Bluffs to be collected and stored for selling.

Bronx Zoo Bug Carousel

The Bug Carousel at the Bronx Zoo is located next to the Butterfly Garden. Instead of the traditional horses one would normally find on a carousel, this carousel features 64 different insects for riders to choose from. It also includes two stationary chariots, a monarch butterfly, and a dung beetle.

The ride was established in 2005 and has become a staple of every child's visit to the zoo. The carousel is both educational and fun. Riders can observe painted murals featuring caterpillars transforming into butterflies running along the circumference of the central pole. The music of the carousel was composed from the sounds insects make.

Best Time to Visit: This carousel is open year round.

Pass/Permit/Fees: The carousel is an additional $6 with a limited-admission ticket.

Closest City or Town: Bronx

Physical Address:
Bug Carousel
Crotona Parkway
Bronx, NY 10460

GPS Coordinates: 40.84949° N, 73.87980° W

Did You Know? Each insect mount is hand carved from basswood and painted to match its real-life counterpart.

Untermyer Park

Untermyer Park and Gardens is located on the hill where the Greystone Estate used to sit. Samuel Untermyer purchased the estate in 1899. He was very passionate about flowers and gardening. Over the course of the 41 years that he lived there, he employed many gardeners and added more greenhouses to the ones established by the previous owner. His gardens were well-known throughout the country, and he would occasionally open them to the public to allow people to visit and enjoy their splendor. When he passed, 43 acres of the original 150 were gifted to Yonkers. After this acquisition, the gardens sat pretty much abandoned for years. However, the gardens have been under repair by the Untermyer Gardens Conservancy since 2011.

Best Time to Visit: The best time to visit is during summer when the gardens are in full bloom.

Pass/Permit/Fees: There is no fee associated with this location.

Closest City or Town: Yonkers

Physical Address:
Untermyer Park and Gardens
945 N. Broadway
Yonkers, NY 10701

GPS Coordinates: 40.97819° N, 73.88803° W

Did You Know? In the 1970s, Untermyer Park was the site of seances and Satanic rituals, earning it the nickname "Devil's Hole" with the locals.

Proper Planning

With this guide, you are well on your way to properly planning a marvelous adventure. When you plan your travels, you should become familiar with the area, save any maps to your phone for access without internet, and bring plenty of water—especially during the summer months. Depending on which adventure you choose, you will also want to bring snacks or even a lunch. For younger children, you should do your research and find destinations that best suit your family's needs. You should also plan when and where to get gas, local lodgings, and food. We've done our best to group these destinations based on nearby towns and cities to help make planning easier.

Dangerous Wildlife

There are several dangerous animals and insects you may encounter while hiking. With a good dose of caution and awareness, you can explore safely. Here are steps you can take to keep yourself and your loved ones safe from dangerous flora and fauna while exploring:

- Keep to the established trails.
- Do not look under rocks, leaves, or sticks.
- Keep hands and feet out of small crawl spaces, bushes, covered areas, or crevices.
- Wear long sleeves and pants to keep arms and legs protected.
- Keep your distance should you encounter any dangerous wildlife or plants.

Do not rely on cell service for navigation or emergencies. Always have a map with you and let someone know where you are and how long you intend to be gone, just in case.

First Aid Information

Always travel with a first aid kit in case of emergencies.

Here are items you should be certain to include in your primary first aid kit:

- Nitrile gloves
- Blister care products
- Band-Aids in multiple sizes and waterproof type
- Ace wrap and athletic tape
- Alcohol wipes and antibiotic ointment
- Irrigation syringe
- Tweezers, nail clippers, trauma shears, safety pins
- Small zip-lock bags containing contaminated trash

It is recommended to also keep a secondary first aid kit, especially when hiking, for more serious injuries or medical emergencies. Items in this should include:

- Blood clotting sponges
- Sterile gauze pads
- Trauma pads

- Second-skin/burn treatment
- Triangular bandages/sling
- Butterfly strips
- Tincture of benzoin
- Medications (ibuprofen, acetaminophen, antihistamine, aspirin, etc.)
- Thermometer
- CPR mask
- Wilderness medicine handbook
- Antivenin

There is much more to explore, but this is a great start.

For information on all national parks, visit https://www.nps.gov/index.htm .

This site will give you information on up-to-date entrance fees and how to purchase a park pass for unlimited access to national and state parks. This site will also introduce you to all of the trails at each park.

Always check before you travel to destinations to make sure there are no closures. Some hiking trails close when there is heavy rain or snow in the area and other parks close parts of their land for the migration of wildlife. Attractions may change their hours or temporarily shut down for various reasons. Check the websites for the most up-to-date information.

Printed in Great Britain
by Amazon

19795303R00081